POWER

THOUGHTS

for TEENS AND

YOUNG ADULTS

365 days of empowered thinking

JACOB GLASS

DEDICATION TO:

Doug Nale and Jill Messick

Introduction and How to Use This Book

Actually, you can use this book any way you want to because it is now YOUR book. I place it in your hands to make use of in whatever way best serves you.

Please do USE it and make it your own. Each daily reading is a template for you to use, so feel free to change the words in any way that makes YOU feel better. I have not spoken down to you in any way or changed my own language. I know you are smart. You know how to look up a word you may not understand. You are awesome that way and in so many other ways. I trust you.

Also, you do not have to read the book in order. You can just "plop" it open each day and read whatever page you land on. You could start on the last page and read it from ending to beginning – there really is no order to the lessons. You may read more than one page per day or stay on the same page for a few days. I do strongly suggest that you read the page out loud to yourself – several times is good to let it really sink into your mind and make it your own.

I use the word God and Source and Universe, but feel free to change that to whatever words you prefer. This book has no particular religion or theology to it at all. It is about universal truths rather than any particular dogma.

I wrote the book I would have wanted someone to have written for me as a teenager – one that would have saved me a lot of time and anguish. I had a LOT of fear and anxiety all through my youth and well into adulthood. I was bullied in school and there was violence and abuse in my home while growing up. I lived in almost constant fear for many many years. I had extremely low self-esteem and chronic physical conditions that were the result of a lot of stress and anxiety. Adding to this was a great deal of death and loss, including the death of my sister, parents, grandparents, cousins, school mates and loved ones.

My teen years were not fun or fruitful because I did not have anyone to teach me HOW TO THINK. School gave me a lot of facts and figures and some skills – but the skill I believe we all need most in this life has to do with teaching us how to think in ways that are helpful to us in our everyday lives. This book is my attempt to help you help yourself - to guide your own thinking in ways that will help you the rest of your life. I'm not perfect. This book is not perfect. Humans are not perfect. But the GREAT news is that we don't need to be perfect in order to be happy, peaceful and thrive in life. We don't need perfect parents or circumstances either. We can take whatever we have right now and make the best of it so that it gets better and better and better by making our mind our best friend instead of our worst enemy. The journey starts here. May you find great help in this book and if you do, share it with others. You may even want to start a small group of readers to form a "Power Thoughts for Teens and Young Adults" study group to support each other. There is power in joining with others and ideas grow stronger when they are shared.

<u>You are amazing</u>.

p.s. You will see that I have capitalized some words that are not normally capitalized. This is to denote Divine Nature.

Epigraph

"The roses under my window make no reference to former roses or better ones; they are what they are; they exist with God today. There is no time to them. There is simply the rose; it is perfect in every moment of its existence."

Ralph Waldo Emerson

"You are altogether irreplaceable in the Mind of God. No one else can fill your part in it, and while you leave your part of it empty your eternal place merely waits for your return."

Helen Schucman

ACKNOWLEDGMENTS

Everyone everywhere.

POWER THOUGHTS
for
TEENS &
YOUNG ADULTS

POWER THOUGHT #1

There is nothing wrong with me.

There is nothing about me that needs to be fixed.

I am a Divine Creation of God and I deserve to live

and experience the best that life has to offer today.

There is no one just like me in the entire world.

I am a wonderful unique creation and

I am happy to be just who I am.

I allow others to be who they are and

I know that this is a Universe of wonderful diversity.

I appreciate others, because I appreciate myself.

We are all unique and yet in many ways the same.

There is no competition, no pressure to conform.

I love and appreciate myself and others today.

POWER THOUGHT #2

I am loved and supported by Source today.

I have a Divine Intuition within me that guides me

to make all the best choices for myself today.

I am making good choices today that lift me up

and guide me to a joyous present and future.

All things are possible for me because

I am a Child of God and am loved beyond measure.

I look forward to a day of joyous miracles unfolding

before me as I hold to my own Center within

and make the choices that will bear good fruit.

Today I seek and receive God's Guidance to

help me make the choices that will lead me to

a bright and happy future.

P O W E R T H O U G H T #3

I see the good in life today.

I see the good in myself and in all those I meet.

I do not compare myself with anyone else

or with the culture around me.

I am not competing with anyone for

there is only one me in the entire world!

I am not auditioning for a part

because I got the part of wonderful me!

I am seeing the good in life and in myself today.

POWER THOUGHT #4

I am not afraid to ask for help when I need it.

Everyone needs help from time to time and

it is not weak to ask for help.

If I don't know the answer, it's not because

I am stupid or lazy or not good enough.

I can simply ask for as much help as I need

to learn at my own unique pace, in my own way.

I have courage and boldness in asking for help,

and I know that I am able to help others

who may need it today too.

None of us is on our own.

I am not alone.

We are all in this together.

There is help for me if I am willing

to ask for and receive it.

P O W E R   T H O U G H T   # 5

I am not responsible for my parents' choices.

I am not responsible for the decisions my

friends or family make.

I can love & accept others without agreeing with them.

I cannot save anyone – I can only love them as they are.

I am only responsible for my own choices in life.

I am learning to make healthy decisions for myself as

I continue to learn and grow as a person.

I know that as I make healthy loving choices for myself,

I may inspire others through my example.

I release myself from being anxious about what

other people are choosing or doing as

I focus my attention on making good choices

that will help me to grow in love, strength and joy.

POWER THOUGHT #6

Life responds quickly to my positive thoughts today.

I am loving and kind and I see love all around me as

I walk the path of Grace and gently unfolding good.

I release all fear and resistance and

I trust Life to guide and direct my day with joyful ease.

I cannot fail to be at the right place at the right time

as I show up, prepared, on time, doing what I said

I would do, with a good attitude.

Life loves and supports me today.

POWER THOUGHT #7

I am focused on progress, not perfection.

Perfection is a stressful myth that doesn't help me.

Instead, I choose to focus on every little bit of

progress I make each day as I do my best.

My best today cannot be compared to the

best of anyone else, or even to what my best

was yesterday, or last week, or last year.

I am focused on going _in the right direction_

instead of comparing myself to an unrealistic ideal

of perfection which only makes me feel bad.

I am celebrating my progress today by

focusing on every tiny step forward I have taken so far.

I focus on progress, not perfection.

POWER THOUGHT #8

I am a lovable person and I deserve to live
in joy and to have my dreams come true.
God created me as worthy and there is
nothing that I need to do to earn
the limitless love of God.
I am lovable because I exist.

POWER THOUGHT #9

I matter, and my life matters.

I came here to the planet to make a positive difference

by being myself and expressing my gifts and talents.

No one can be me and no one can take my place.

I am an important part of the Cosmic Plan of Life.

Without me, there is something very wonderful

and magical missing in the world.

I continue to learn and grow and find my place

in this wonderful plan for the expansion of good here.

There is no hurry about this.

It is a great adventure and I am enjoying the process

of finding out all the wonderful ways that

I can contribute to the world by sharing

who and what I am in my own unique ways.

I matter, and my life matters.

POWER THOUGHT # 10

If for any reason I have a stressful day or moment

I am able to let go of it when I arrive home

or at any time I choose to release it.

I simply take a little time for myself to sit,

close my eyes, take some deep breaths as

I release the day or situation behind me.

I can quietly say or think to myself,

"I am letting go of the day now.

I am letting go of this upset now.

I am letting go of the past now.

I am letting go of stress and worry now.

I release this into the hands of God.

I choose to return to inner peace

as I open my heart and relax my mind."

Then, I continue to breathe and relax

as I feel it floating away from me

like clouds passing by on a windy day.

POWER THOUGHT #11

There is a Power and a Presence guiding my day.

This Presence only loves and knows nothing of limitation.

In It I live and move and exist.

I relax into the Universal Arms today and

allow my good to flow freely and abundantly.

There is no one to impress – nothing to compete for.

There is more than enough good for

all to thrive in the Light.

I open to receive the gifts of God today as Life unfolds

a day of perfect order, beauty and all that is good.

I am blessed and I am a blessing.

All is well.

POWER THOUGHT #12

There is no such thing as "normal."

Fitting in is something sponges can do.

I am not a sponge. I am a wonderful human being.

I can be my own unique self, even if the world

calls it weird or unusual.

The greatest people in history were judged

and criticized by many people.

I know that there is greatness in me too.

I am on my own perfect path and

whether I have many friends or none right now,

I am my own brand of "normal."

As I accept and love myself,

I will attract others who love and accept me.

I am wonderful and unique.

I will find my way as I go.

There is no hurry.

POWER THOUGHT #13

Nothing can delay nor block

my good today except a limiting thought.

I now dissolve all limiting beliefs and ideas, knowing that

I live in a lavishly abundant Universe of endless possibilities.

I stretch out my arms and open my heart today to receive.

The Creative Force of Life is now flowing through me and

everything I need to know is revealed to me as

as I align myself with this Creative Intelligence.

My thoughts are creative and

my words are containers for Power.

I think and speak my world into being today and

I expect a day of peace, joy and ease as

I relax into the Power that effortlessly creates galaxies.

I am thinking thoughts of my limitless good today.

POWER THOUGHT #14

I am not my mistakes.

I am not defined by what I do or don't do.

I say who I am, and I am a work-in-progress.

My mistakes are a part of my growing process

and they help me to know what works and what doesn't.

I am still a valuable person, no matter what.

I can apologize, make amends, and move on.

I let go of my past errors and ask God to

guide me to do better in the future.

I ask for and receive forgiveness now.

I forgive myself and let go of

guilt, blame and shame as I move forward.

I am learning and growing every day.

POWER THOUGHT #15

What others think of me is none of my business.

I am not here to get approval from the world.

I approve of myself.

I am not curious about what anyone is thinking or saying

about me or about the choices I make.

Life is very fun when I let go of trying to please others.

I pursue the things that I love and feel passionate about,

and I allow others to do the same.

I did not come to the planet to run for "most liked."

I came here to express who I am and to enjoy the journey.

I am letting go of what others think about me

because I think I am pretty awesome.

POWER THOUGHT #16

My family is not my source.

I love my family and we support each other,

but God is my limitless Source.

I can be or do or have the life I choose

and it doesn't matter whether my family is rich or poor.

It doesn't matter where I live or what the

other people around me are being, doing or having.

All things are possible for me as I go

directly to the Source to lead and guide me to success.

God has limitless good and my job is to

know that nothing good is being withheld from me.

As a Child of God, I have limitless resources.

I am open to receive the limitless gifts of

my Divine Father-Mother today and every day.

<u>P O W E R   T H O U G H T   # 17</u>

I can choose my own thoughts.

I don't have to believe every thought in my head.

I can choose the thoughts that are loving, positive,

and that feel good when I think them.

I choose to let go of attack thoughts about

myself and anyone else.

I let go of stressful thoughts and

replace them with loving peaceful thoughts.

I treat my mind like a wonderful puppy that

needs to be gently trained every day.

I am not at the effect of my thoughts.

I have a wonderful mind that I must train every day.

I am training my mind every time I choose

to think life-affirming thoughts.

POWER THOUGHT #18

I am writing the story of my life every day.

I write it by the way I describe it to myself and others.

I can tell a story of "poor me" or

I can tell a story of "lucky me."

Whatever I focus on, and however I tell my story,

I will get more and more of that in my world.

I do not have to be phony or deny that

I have problems or have had pain in my life,

but I can choose to focus on the positive more

than on the things that have hurt me.

If I am sharing my problems or pain,

I can do it as a way of sharing my heart

and not as a way of bringing myself down.

Today, I am writing the story of lucky me

as I focus on what I am grateful for

because I am alive and it is a new day

with new opportunities to expand my good.

<u>P O W E R   T H O U G H T   # 19</u>

I have a wonderful heart that is full of love.

Everyone has problems and challenges in their life.

It's impossible to tell from looking at someone

what is really going on inside of them.

I care about other people and love to help when I can.

I will not judge others because I have no idea what

is really going on inside of them or in the

privacy of their own homes.

They may look like they have the perfect life,

but they may suffer in private every day.

I choose to keep my heart open today

so that I can give and receive love

wherever I go and whatever I am doing.

I am a loving person and I am looking

at others with kindness and love today.

POWER THOUGHT # 20

If I am sad, if I am hurt, if I am lonely or in despair,

if I forget Who I am, or am filled with shame or regret,

if I am lost or overwhelmed and confused, if I lose my way,

if I feel sick, or wounded, or gripped by fear, if I feel

abandoned, weak, deprived or that I am not enough,

if I feel that I cannot go on, or do not know

which way to turn – I do not need to

withdraw from the world to hide from life.

I can turn to my Creator and let myself be held in Grace.

I can remember that this too shall pass and that

I <u>will</u> smile and laugh again.

In my greatest weakness, God's Presence is strong in me.

In my darkest night, God's Light is shining in me.

In my deepest loss, God's Grace is holding me.

POWER THOUGHT #21

I am staying in my own mental yard today.

I am minding my own business and doing my own thing.

Everyone wins in my space, including me.

In Spirit, there is no size, no comparison, no order of

difficulty. There is nothing to prove, no one to impress.

I release all desire to be special, for God created me and

there is nothing I need add to make myself more valuable.

I am happily playing in my own yard.

I now give 100% of my attention to those who love,

appreciate and support me just as I am.

I only spend time with those it feels great to be around.

I withdraw all attention from those who don't get me, don't

like me, don't approve of me, or want me to be different.

I release them with love and turn entirely away from them

and I now only attract and spend time where there is

mutual love, support and great joy. There is no one and

nothing to audition for – I've got the part of ME and I am

playing it with great ease and joy as I savor all my own

unique weirdness here in my own yard.

POWER THOUGHT #22

#DDHD

Dreams don't have deadlines.

Some people excel at a very early age and

others succeed further down the road.

So what?

I will continue to have dreams and goals

as long as I live and there is no race to the end.

I give myself whatever time it takes to

continue dreaming new dreams and

moving in their direction.

I never give up on myself because tomorrow is

another new day to experience joy whether

I think I am making progress or not.

The greatest success in life is JOY anyhow.

The more I am experiencing joy in the moment,

the more successful I already am.

POWER THOUGHT #23

I live in a Friendly Universe, which responds to my vibration.

My thoughts, words, attitudes and actions

are the seeds I sow.

I will harvest in abundance just what I plant,

nothing more or less than that.

I choose today to sow seeds of joy, kindness,

love and abundance.

I sow laughter, optimism, warmth, goodness and mercy.

There is nothing for me to get –

I merely harvest my own crops.

I release all struggle, striving, manipulation and control.

I trust the Universe today to respond to my loving energy

as I walk in Grace and peace, sharing my Light with

those who are open to receive it.

All is well in me and in my world for this is

a day of Divine Harvest and happy sowing.

POWER THOUGHT #24

I am not missing out on anything.

Wherever I am right now is the right place for the moment.

Instead of focusing on where others are and what

is happening in other places, I focus on making

the best of where I am right now.

My life is happening now, not later.

My life is happening here, not elsewhere.

I make the best of things, not the worst of things.

I can enjoy myself because I enjoy my own company.

I am learning to make friends with myself.

P O W E R   T H O U G H T   #25

Instead of making mental lists of what I think is

wrong with me, I make lists of what is right with me.

I can love and accept myself even when I am in

the process of making positive changes in my behavior.

There is no reason to beat myself up in order to do better.

Instead, I encourage myself as I would a good friend.

It is wonderful when others encourage me,

but that is not their job – it's my job to encourage me.

The more I encourage myself, the farther I can go in life.

And as I encourage others, I am also encouraging myself.

Everything I give out to others, I amplify in myself.

I encourage myself, I encourage others,

and every day I feel better and better and better.

There are many things right with me and

I am reminding myself of that every day.

POWER THOUGHT #26

I am magnetic to my good!

There is a Dynamic Something in the Universe which

responds to my thoughts, words, feelings and attitudes.

Today, I choose to focus on all that is good as

I go on rampages of appreciation and praise.

I TELL people how wonderful they are as

I lift them up – and I tell myself how wonderful I am

as I am lifted up to higher and higher levels of Joy!

I am irresistible to my greater good and

I am gathering up evidence that Life loves me.

My Infinite Source is within me and the blessings are

springing forth from me today in all directions.

I am not worried about the future for

the best is yet to come as I envision only the good.

There is no need for me to make anything happen nor

to be aggressive or pushy, for miracles of love

are opening the doors to my good with Grace and ease.

I remain calm and yet alert as I bless the world and

count up my own blessings while walking this path of Peace.

<u>P O W E R   T H O U G H T   # 27</u>

Love makes my world beautiful today.

As I look through the eyes of love today,

I see a world of beauty and of Light.

I will not focus on the errors in myself or others,

but instead, I will be a detective seeking clues

leading to the innocence, kindness and Grace in us all.

I am shredding all evidence to the contrary as

I dissolve all walls around my heart

and take down all defenses.

Love is my strength today as I open my heart

to receive the Love of God & let it flow through me

to the world around me.

POWER THOUGHT #28

No one can pressure me into doing

something that isn't right for me.

I follow my gut and not the crowd.

There is an inner Voice in me that

I can count on to steer me in the right direction.

I go within daily to consult my own Guidance.

I am stand strong in my own truth and

I only do what I know is right for me.

P O W E R T H O U G H T #29

I do not have to believe every thought

that comes into mind.

I have the freedom to choose which thoughts

to keep and which thoughts to dissolve and release.

Today, I choose the thoughts that create the feelings

I want to feel about myself, my life, my body,

my personality and the world around me.

I am not at the whim of my moods.

I can change my mood by changing my thoughts.

Today, I allow the peace, love and joy of Spirit to guide

and direct me to all that is for my highest good

and greatest expansion.

I have a wonderful present and a brilliant future.

Life loves me and my best years are still ahead of me.

POWER THOUGHT #30

No one can rush me in any relationship.

No one has permission to push me into

making a decision I am not ready to make yet.

I am a powerful person with the right

to choose what I want and when I will make a choice.

I am strong in my "yes" and

strong in my "no."

I get to decide what is right for me,

when I am ready to make the decision.

I take my time to seek guidance from within

and from those I trust and who have my best

interests at heart.

I do my research and decide when I am ready.

I am a powerful chooser.

<u>P O W E R   T H O U G H T   # 31</u>

I am not trying to be cool or to fit in —

I am simply being my wonderful self.

I follow my own internal GPS once

I have decided where I want to go.

Every human being has an internal Guidance System

which leads us in the direction of whatever we are

focusing on at the time.

I choose to focus on the things that uplift me

and light up the joy in me.

I let go of what others are thinking or doing as

I follow my own internal GPS to my greater good today.

<u>P O W E R   T H O U G H T   #32</u>

I walk in peace and loving-kindness today.

The peace of God is mine and I activate it now.

There is no war to fight – no enemy of the Light.

I release and dissolve all attack thoughts, all strategies,

all schemes and resentments and judgments.

Today, I appreciate what already is and

I am not striving to get anything,

or to arrive somewhere different.

I walk in tenderness today and I see a world of

beauty and Light as I am healed in gentle laughter.

All that I do is done with loving non-attachment

as I surrender it all to the Divine Presence within me.

This is a day that unfolds in effortless joyful ease

as I focus on gratitude, praise and appreciation.

There is nothing to fix, or fear, or push against.

All is well in my world.

<u>P O W E R   T H O U G H T   # 33</u>

I breathe in deeply and I am relaxed and at peace.

Nothing wavers me from my truth today as

I stand firmly in the Love and Grace of the Universe.

Nothing disturbs me today and it is impossible

for me to contain the Love that is flowing through me now.

Life rises up to greet me as I walk through the open doors

summoning my good to me through my JOYFUL vibration.

I do not struggle, push against, argue with

or try to make anything happen.

Life is for me and none are against me as I walk in

gentleness and love today.

POWER THOUGHT #34

I walk in perfect Grace today as

I release any tendency to struggle and fight.

I show up, on time, prepared, doing what I said I would do,

with a good attitude, and I walk through

the open doors to my good.

There is no need for me to worry or rush for

I cannot fail to be at the right place at the right time as

I relax into the Divine Plan for this beautiful new day.

In my world, all is well and Life loves me!

POWER THOUGHT #35

I bless my body and I bathe it in Light with
my loving thoughts and feelings today.
This body is an expression of Consciousness and there
is nothing unspiritual or unholy about it in any way.
I do not abuse my body and I do not allow others to
use or abuse it in any way.
I treat my body with love and kindness
in my thoughts, words and actions.

I bless this body just as it is and just as it is not.
It is an extension of my own Creative Imagination and
is my oldest and dearest companion –
I give thanks for this precious friend.

POWER THOUGHT #36

I am a creative person.

I have God-given talents and abilities

I have not even discovered yet.

I am opening up my mind and soul today

to let the Universe flow creative ideas to me.

I can do far more than I yet realize.

I am looking forward to discovering all

the wonderful things I will create in my lifetime.

There is no rush about any of this.

My creativity is unfolding in perfect timing

and in delightful ways as I remember

NOT to argue for my limitations.

I am a creative person and

I have a lot to contribute to the world

as I continue to discover my gifts.

POWER THOUGHT #37

I am worthy and lovable because I exist.

My worth is not about what I do or achieve in life.

I do not have to justify my existence or worth,

because I am a Divine Creation of the Great Spirit.

My talents and abilities are my happy contribution

to the world around me, but they are not

rent paid to the planet.

As a Child of God, I am under Grace and so

I am worthy and valuable simply because I exist.

I do not have to struggle in order to

deserve to live or take up space on the planet.

I joyfully contribute here because of my generous Spirit

and as an expression of the love and gratitude

I feel for the Creator Who made me.

I am worthy and lovable because I exist.

POWER THOUGHT #38

I trust the path I am on and I trust the process of Life.

If I find I am going in the wrong direction,

I can always turn around and get back

on the highlighted route.

I release all attachments to specific outcomes and

if one dreams dies, I simply dream a new dream.

I am always able to dream a new dream for myself.

I keep track of my Joy instead tracking losses and gains.

When the tide goes out, no one calls this a loss or a failure;

therefore I will not judge my own life

by appearances of loss or retreat either.

I know they are temporary.

My true success is in terms of how much

peace and Joy I am allowing myself to experience.

I now relax and allow myself to enjoy the journey

as I appreciate today's gifts.

POWER THOUGHT #39

I have a wonderful mind that serves me well.

My mind is not my enemy and I am not a slave to it.

My mind is my very good friend and

I am learning how to guide it more every day.

I do not compare my mind to that of those around me.

I do not let the media hypnotize me into

thinking the way they want me to.

My mind is not stupid, or lazy, or limited.

My mind is not hyper or damaged or weird.

I have a wonderful mind created by the same Source

that makes the planets revolve around the sun

in perfect proximity and order.

Everyone has negative thoughts and attack thoughts

but I am learning to release those thoughts

and to gently guide my mind back to peace.

I guide my mind in the direction of loving thoughts that

are uplifting, supportive and that feel good

when I think them.

I love and appreciate my beautiful mind.

POWER THOUGHT #40

People love me and I love people.

I am drawing into my life those with whom

I can have the most healthy and joyous relationships.

I don't have to change or be different in order

to have wonderful friends and companions.

I don't have to fit the molds the media presents.

I am creating my own wonderful unique

circle of friends and we lift each other up.

I am interested in relationships in which

we bring out the best in each other, not the worst.

I let go of gossip, competition and jealousy.

I am a very lovable person and

I am attracting more love into my life every day

as I focus on seeing what is good in myself

and those around me.

People love me and I love people.

<u>P O W E R   T H O U G H T</u> #41

I am happy with who and what I am.

I am not here to please others or to force myself

to fit myself into some box the culture created.

I am here to create my own life in my own way.

I allow others to do the same and so

I see my world as a place of co-creating with love & passion.

I am finding my way and there is no race to get there –

there is no finish line to cross or trophy to win.

I am happy with who I am and who I am becoming.

POWER THOUGHT #42

There is no lack of good in my world.

I came from Infinity and I am a Divine Creation.

Therefore, all the resources I need to live a happy life

are available to me from the Source I came from.

I do not have to count on people or companies or

on economies or industries for my good.

They are simply the avenues the Universe may

use to deliver whatever I need into my world.

I am in the receptive mode today and

I am lining up to receive whatever I need today.

I have an Infinite Source of limitless good.

P O W E R   T H O U G H T   #43

Love and Joy are the guiding forces of my life.

I need do nothing to force anything happen for the

Divine Plan of my life operates

through attraction, not promotion.

I follow the Call to Joy instead of the drive of ambition.

My vibration is clear, strong and alive

with prospering power.

I listen to the Guidance of the still small Voice and

I know that God is on the Field.

Today I am walking through the open doors as

I recognize that right where I am, God is, and all is well.

POWER THOUGTHT #44

It's a new day of new Life and new possibilities for good.

I am ready to happily swim, float and

play in the ocean of miracles.

There is nothing limiting me but my own thought

and now all old limiting beliefs are washed away in the

shimmering blue waves.

I am not afraid to be happy today.

I am not afraid of love.

I'm here to experience all the good that Life has

to offer me today as I OPEN TO RECEIVE Its gifts.

I am swimming with life today and Life is very very good.

POWER THOUGHT #45

Right here, right now, no matter what happens in my world,

all things are held perfectly in the hands of God.

From the smallest to the greatest,

everything is illuminated with the Presence.

I will not study or obsess about problems and wounds today

but will instead remember that there is no opposite to God.

There are not two powers in the Universe, but only One,

and in this One, I live and move and have my being.

There is nothing to fear.

<u>POWER THOUGHT #46</u>

I am in the right place at the right time today.

And I always have what I need.

Life loves me and things go well for me.

I am treated with favor everywhere I go

and I live by Grace rather than by struggle.

I need not chase after anything or anyone for

I am a magnet for the best that Life has to offer.

I am sailing along across an ocean of love and possibilities.

I am a grateful Child of God today & all is well with me.

POWER THOUGHT #47

I forgive myself and learn from my mistakes.

There is nothing helpful about guilt or shame.

I can have a healthy remorse for my mistakes

without punishing myself or beating myself up.

I make amends when I have hurt someone by

making a sincere apology and doing whatever

I can to make things right,

but I neither justify my mistake nor

attack myself for not being perfect.

I learn from my mistakes and grow in wisdom

as I look to see what my lesson is,

and then forgive myself and let it go.

<u>POWER THOUGHT #48</u>

I don't have to have all the answers.

My parents don't have to have all the answers.

Life is a journey of discovery for us all and

we can learn together through joy instead of pain

by being patient and understanding.

We are all in this together and no one is

better, superior, less-than, or inferior to anyone else.

Today, I am focusing on how the Universe continues

to create great variety and diversity in all creatures.

We are all learning and growing together so

today I choose to open my heart with kindness,

seeing that even the most lost soul is trying

to find their own way in this world.

I have compassion and tolerance for myself

and all those I see today knowing that

we are all in this together.

<u>P O W E R   T H O U G H T   # 49</u>

There is no competition, criticism nor

condemnation in me, nor towards me.

There is more than enough good for all of us to thrive.

Everyone wins in my space, including me.

I walk and live in an atmosphere of joyful success

and all around me Life reflects my Consciousness

as my days unfold in effortlessly happy ways.

I am prepared to be delighted by Life today.

POWER THOUGHT #50

I am learning to take good care of myself.

I am in the process of finding out what works best for me.

I am affected by the things I put in my mouth and

even more so by what comes out of my mouth.

I love myself, therefore, I am taking responsibility

for treating myself with kindness and respect all the time.

I cannot expect anyone to treat me better

than I treat myself because I am the one setting the tone.

Today, I am making the choices that will show

love, kindness and respect for myself.

P O W E R   T H O U G H T   #51

I invest in the people I love by finding out

what matters to them and what makes them feel good.

Instead of giving them what I would want,

I give them what THEY want as a sign of my caring.

I love it when someone takes the time & interest

to find out what I love and care about,

and so I do the same for those I want to be close to.

I am learning how to be a master of love

by giving people what matters to them.

POWER THOUGHT #52

I speak words of admiration and appreciation today.

I realize that most of the world is starving for love

and so today I am feeding the people in my world

with words of encouragement and support.

I no longer take anyone for granted.

I speak words of love and appreciation to my family

without embarrassment today.

I am showing my love more every day

as I speak words of appreciation to those in my world.

<u>POWER THOUGHT #53</u>

I give my attention to those who love and approve of me

instead of those who criticize or judge me.

I am not here to win a popularity contest.

I am here to enjoy my journey through life by

expressing myself and going where the love is.

I walk through the open doors instead of

trying to get in where I am not wanted or welcome.

As I practice loving and approving of myself,

I attract others who love and approve of me NOW,

just as I am, and just as I am not.

I give my attention to those who love and accept me.

POWER THOUGHT #54

There is no one just like me in the whole world.
I don't compare myself with what others are
being, doing or having in their lives because
I did not come to earth to just duplicate what
everyone else has chosen.
Others may inspire me and activate my
own creativity, but we are unique expressions
of the one Universal Substance.
There is no one to compare myself to
because I am an original creation.
There is no one just like me in the whole world
and I am an amazing work-in-progress.

P O W E R T H O U G H T #55

Everything is working out well for me today.

I trust that the Power that holds galaxies in place,

turns seeds into flowers and makes the planets

revolve around the sun in perfect proximity

can also guide and direct me to my greater good.

I am trusting that the Universe is a friendly place

and that Life loves and supports me today.

Everything is working out well for me today.

POWER THOUGHT #56

Today I will not condemn myself or

anyone in my world.

I know that everyone is doing the best they can

with the information and wisdom they

currently have, including myself.

I can discern if something is right for me

or not, and even see where someone else

may be making wrong choices without

going into condemnation and attack thoughts.

I keep my heart open today and my mind

free of condemnation and attack.

I live and let live as

I focus on making loving choices for myself.

POWER THOUGHT #57

I persevere in the face of challenges.

I don't give up on myself or on my dreams

just because there are obstacles or problems.

I don't get down on myself or give in to anger or despair.

If I need to take a break and step back for a while,

I allow myself the freedom to do so.

If I need help or guidance, I ask for it.

I am not weak or helpless or stupid,

and I also am not in a race to a mountaintop.

I can persevere at my own pace knowing that

as I persist with a good attitude,

everything is unfolding for me in the

perfect time-space sequence for me to

move through the challenges of life.

POWER THOUGHT #58

I believe in myself and in my dreams.

My subconscious mind is a powerful ally

in helping me to accomplish wonderful things in life.

Because my mind is one with the Universal Source

of all wisdom, I have access to limitless possibilities.

I can turn any problem over to my subconscious

mind and allow it to orchestrate the answer for me.

I am giving any problems today to my beautiful mind

to resolve for me and I am staying relaxed yet alert,

knowing the right answers will come to me

in the perfect timing and perfect ways.

POWER THOUGHT #59

My mind is my good friend and servant.

It awaits my direction on what to think about and focus on.

I rule my mind, which I alone must rule.

I choose to rule with love, joy, peace and kindness today.

I focus on the thoughts and aspects of life

that stimulate JOY in me.

I am not waiting for life or other people

or God to make me happy.

I love that I get to choose how good I want to feel by

focusing my mind on the POSITIVE ASPECTS of

whatever and whoever is in my world today.

My heart is open, my mind is clear, my spirit is renewed

and everything I need comes to me today

in ease, joy and Grace!

POWER THOUGHT #60

I am blessed by the Thoughts of God today.

Wherever I go, Angels light the way with messages of

Love, peace, power, healing and beauty.

I am surrendering to the Divine Plan for my

happiness and greater good as I walk in Love today.

I remember that I am safe, that all is well, and that

all things are held perfectly in the hands of God.

As I breathe this in, my body and mind relax

and I cannot help but smile as I melt into Divine Love.

P O W E R   T H O U G H T # 61

I am enough just as I am.

What others think of me is none of my business.

I have a unique voice in the world and

I am going to use it to express my truth.

I am not afraid to speak out and

say what I think.

I do my best to speak with kindness and

without attack or defensiveness.

I release others to do the same.

I AM ENOUGH AND I AM NOT AFRAID TO BE ME.

POWER THOUGHT #62

I am worthy of love and companionship.

My energy attracts wonderful people into my life

and we cheer each other on every day.

There is no competition, criticism or jealousy

between us because there is more than enough

good to go around for us all.

I am attracting wonderful people into my life

and I open my heart today to give and receive love freely.

POWER THOUGHT #63

I appreciate the beauty around me today.

I take time today to notice beauty wherever I find it.

I slow down enough to look up and appreciate

the sky, the trees, the birds of the air.

I look down to see the beauty of even a small

blade of grass growing through a sidewalk crack.

I particularly take time to appreciate my own beauty

as a beloved Child of God, of the Universe.

The more I appreciate life, the more there is to appreciate.

POWER THOUGHT #64

All the right doors are opening for me now.

I don't need to smash my head against the doors

that are closed or locked before me.

I am not auditioning for life or for approval.

My good is seeking me as I am seeking it.

We find each other at the perfect time and

in perfect ways as I stay open and

connected to my Divine Source.

The right doors open before me and

I walk through with joy and ease today.

P O W E R T H O U G H T # 65

The thoughts I think and the words I speak

are creating my world for me today and for tomorrow.

I choose to create the best by expecting only good to come.

I love and honor myself because I am a child of God,

therefore I deserve and accept only that which reflects

my Divine Inheritance and I am OPEN TO RECEIVE it now.

POWER THOUGHT #66

I am an abundant prosperous person

and money flows to me with ease.

God is the Source of all resources

so my Source is God, not people or even money.

I am a money magnet and I use money wisely.

I have integrity and I know how to let money

work for me as I save some, spend some and share some.

I love to play the money game and

I know that money loves to come to me.

I AM AN ABUNDANT PROSPEROUS PERSON.

P O W E R   T H O U G H T   # 67

Life loves me and is seeking me out to bless today.

I open my heart, my mind and my hands today to receive

the blessings of God as I allow Grace to

guide me through the open doors.

I gently share my blessings all those who are open to

receive me and the gifts I have to give

through the Presence within me.

Life loves me and love pursues me.

<u>P O W E R   T H O U G H T # 68</u>

I have courage and confidence in myself.

I am a powerful being and I am growing

more powerful and loving every day.

Love is the greatest power in the Universe

and my love makes me strong and courageous.

I pursue my dreams and goals with the

courage and confidence of a champion.

Even when I lose, I am growing and learning

more about how to do better in the future.

I love the person I am becoming.

P O W E R   T H O U G H T # 69

No one has permission to touch me

unless I give it to them.

I honor my body and I do not use it to try

to get love or approval from anyone.

My body is sacred and is a vessel of my Eternal Spirit.

I treat it with kindness, love and respect.

If anyone speaks disrespectfully about it,

I walk away and don't look back.

I don't even give it another thought.

I only go where I am loved, honored and respected.

I hold not grudges or resentments – I move on

to the place where I am appreciated as I am.

I do not negotiate with my body.

I am strong in who I am and if someone

cannot respect my boundaries, they are not

welcome in my life.

I respect my body and I respect myself.

P O W E R T H O U G H T # 70

I am not afraid of rejection.

Successful people get rejected all the time.

It doesn't stop me or dishearten me.

I simply move on and try elsewhere.

I put myself out there and go for what I want.

If I am rejected, I know that I am being spared

from something or someone that was not a good match.

I persist in moving forward and don't let myself

get caught up in self-pity or victim thinking.

I know that as I persist, I will succeed.

Successful people like me are not afraid of rejection.

<u>P O W E R   T H O U G H T #71</u>

There is no criticism, competition nor condemnation

in me nor towards me.

Everyone wins in my space, including me!

Divine Love is drawing to me now all that is needed

to make me happy and make my life complete.

This a miraculous joyous day and I cannot wait

to see how Spirit handles every little detail perfectly!

<u>POWER THOUGHT #72</u>

I cannot control what other people, or the world,

says or does – I can only control myself.

Therefore, I must guard my mind from

negative stinkin thinkin.

I can choose the thoughts I want to think.

I will not let anything steal my joy today.

I choose to focus my attention on

what I love and appreciate.

I let everyone off the hook today, including myself.

I let upsetting things roll right off my back.

I am in charge of my thoughts and beliefs

and I choose to focus on only the good today.

POWER THOUGHT #73

I am watching my words today.

I know that words can hurt or heal –

they can lift up, or tear down.

I want to be one who inspires and uplifts

with the words I speak in this world.

I won't let myself get caught up

in gossip or criticism because it

ultimately makes me feel horrible.

I know that whatever I put out into the world

comes back to me multiplied, including my words.

I am carefully choosing the right words today

that will sow seeds which will bring me

a good and happy harvest of empowering good feelings.

P O W E R   T H O U G H T   #74

I am putting first things first in my life now as

I take time today to think about what is important.

I know it is not enough to say that certain things are

important to me –

I must show it through my

daily actions and by showing up.

I make time for the people I love.

I keep my promises.

I am showing up, prepared, on time,

doing what I said I would do, with a good attitude.

If I say family is most important to me,

I schedule specific times with them.

If I say my health matters,

I schedule time to take care of my health.

My actions and my words are matching up these days and

it is creating a life of joy, peace and deep satisfaction.

POWER THOUGHT #75

I encourage and uplift those around me.

I don't take people for granted.

I thank my parents and teachers and siblings

for anything and everything they do for me.

I ask them if they need my help and

I happily give it whenever I can.

I give them sincere compliments frequently

and let them know I see how wonderful they are.

I think of more than just myself – I think of others too.

I let go of focusing on what I don't like about others,

and instead focus on their positive aspects.

The more I focus on and talk about what I like

about someone, the more there is to like about them.

The more I appreciate and uplift others,

the better I feel and the more there is to appreciate.

POWER THOUGHT #76

I surrender to the Grace and Peace of God today as

I practice gentle kindness with myself

in all my thoughts and actions.

As I am kind and loving with myself,

I am kind and loving with others.

I walk in God's Love today and I know that

I always have what I need.

I will do my best and let go of the rest.

No matter what happens today,

I know that I am held in Light and all is well.

POWER THOUGHT #77

My body is my dearest oldest friend.

I do not compare it with other bodies.

This is the body God made for me and

I appreciate and honor it as a Divine Creation.

Today I accept and bless my body just as it is, and

just as it is not. I meet it where it is.

I do not punish, abuse, pound or resent my body.

I lovingly speak and think of every single part of it and

I speak TO IT with loving words. I pay attention to it and

have no fear, guilt or shame about it.

I move my body with love today and respect it as a dear

close friend who serves me as best it can each day.

I love and appreciate my beautiful body.

POWER THOUGHT #78

I will not compare my insides to the outsides of

someone else who looks like they have it all together.

Pictures and social media are only "appearances"

and do not tell the real story or mean anything.

I do not play the game of "compare and despair."

I am a unique creation and I have my own path to walk.

What others are thinking or doing with their lives

is none of my business and is outside of my own yard.

I focus on taking care of my own yard and

on making the very best of what is going on here & now.

Everyone has problems and challenges no matter

what it may look like from the outside.

I can be happy only by taking care of my own thinking

and by focusing on what I have to be thankful for

instead of on what I think it missing in my life.

Today, I stay focused on taking care of my own yard

and I let others do the same.

<u>P O W E R T H O U G H T #79</u>

Good morning Lord! It is another day of miracles and light.

I open my heart to receive the gifts of God and

to share my light with the world around me.

There is nothing for me to fear because I am

always guided and protected by Divine Consciousness.

This is a day of unexpected good and blessings.

My joy is rising and my peace is sustained by Source.

POWER THOUGHT #80

I can place my future in the hands of God

and know that I will be guided and helped

to make good decisions and to walk in Grace.

I do not give in to peer pressure if my gut

tells me that something is not good for me.

I know that God is my Source, not some

group or some person who has their own agenda.

I love myself and therefore I do not terrify myself

about the past, present or future.

I don't let anyone or anything sway me from listening to

the Voice of God within me because I trust that Voice.

I am walking in Truth and safety today as

I place my life in the hands of God.

POWER THOUGHT #81

God loves me totally, right now, just as I am.

There is nothing I need to do to be worthy.

This vessel of Light is very worthy indeed.

Today I am a confident Child of God, going forth

to live in joy, abundance, peace, health and love.

P O W E R   T H O U G H T   #82

I am a spiritual being in a spiritual Universe.

The Universe is responding to my Consciousness

and so I have the power to focus my mind on

that which brings more joy and more life to me.

I deliberately and lovingly select the thoughts

that will bring the most good into my world today.

POWER THOUGHT #83

I deliberately select my thoughts as carefully as
I would choose a precious gem at the most
expensive jewelry store in the world.
My thoughts are more valuable than any treasure
the world can offer because they create my world.
These are the precious jewel thoughts I select today:

_____

_____

_____

_____

_____

_____

_____

<u>P O W E R   T H O U G H T S # 84</u>

There is no such thing as normal.

Normal is a myth used by the culture to torture us.

Even in all the ways humans are the same,

we are all also unique and have our own

way of living and walking the Earth.

There is no "normal" family or person.

We did not come to the planet to just do

what the majority are doing if it does not

feel good or natural to us.

My family and life is the one that is right for me and us.

As long as I am coming from love, I'm doing well.

TV and movie families are fictional stories.

There is no such thing as a "reality" show either.

Those people are acting for the camera.

It is not real.

I am not trying to chase the myth of normal because

I would rather be NATURAL – to live the life that

is natural for ME to live.

If it looks "normal" to others, that's fine.

If not, that's cool too.

POWER THOUGHT #85

I am not here to meet the expectations of others.

I am not here to fix a broken world.

I came to express my own unique loving spirit

while in a human physical form.

I am an important being and I recognize

that everyone is equally important.

There are no special people.

We are all unique Divine Creations

and no one is more important than another.

We are all the multi-colored threads in

the Master Tapestry of the Universe.

My expression is important to the whole.

Without me, just as I am,

something important is

missing from the world.

Being myself is what I am here to do.

POWER THOUGHT # 86

There is no limit to what I can achieve in this life.

I have growing faith and confidence in myself

and in my abilities as I learn from my teachers and mentors.

I encourage myself daily and I believe in myself

more every day as I grow and change.

If no one else is encouraging me or believes in me

right now, I am not bitter or resentful about it.

I know that as I encourage myself,

I will attract others who will also believe in me.

I will draw to me those who can help me

and teach me what I need to know to succeed

and to be a person of integrity, love and honor.

I can do whatever I set my mind to and

I believe that whatever lessons and challenges

are before me, I will be able to handle with

the help of the Divine Presence within me.

I am looking forward to seeing how

it all unfolds in the days and years to come!

POWER THOUGHT #87

I am now conducting a fearless searching miracle inventory.

I am looking for the evidence of how I am getting it right

and how love is increasing in my life every day.

I am a Special Agent of the Spiritual Underground

seeking out the clues to the existence of miracles in my life.

This is an ongoing mission and every day I get better and

better at recognizing the hand of God in my world.

This is the most exciting time of my life so far

AND I AM FILLED WITH GRATITUDE AND WONDER.

POWER THOUGHT #88

Wonderful ideas come to me when I quiet my mind

and listen to the Divine Source within me.

I take time every day to sit and let go of stress

as I breathe in peace and Universal Light.

I have access to the limitless wisdom of the Universe

when I grow still and consult the Higher Authority of Source.

Every day I become more focused on the good.

Every day I feel more connected to my Source.

It's almost magical how spending this quiet time

in contemplation and listening then seems to

open doors and opportunities for my greater good.

As I turn within daily and listen, my world is lit by miracles.

POWER THOUGHTS #89

I am entirely ready for God to joyfully use and bless me
through daily miracles and to increase the manifestations of
good in me as I go about my life here on earth.
I have humbly yet boldly asked God to remove
my limiting beliefs and any habit of playing small
or in letting resistance stop me from thriving
and enjoying my life every day.
I am a miracle worker and this is a day
of Divine Harvest in my world.

<u>P O W E R   T H O U G H T</u> #90

I am creating an ongoing gratitude list of all those who have

been a part of these loving miraculous enchantments of

co-creating with God-Source.

I have also made a list of where I have been helpful to

others because it feels so good to

let God joyfully use me every day.

I am a grateful giver and receiver today and

I look forward to watching miracles unfold for us.

Thank You God for the wonders

and delights coming my way.

POWER THOUGHT #91

The cells of my body are constantly renewed

with health and vitality, and my body knows

how to balance itself as I treat it with love.

I do not criticize my body for any reason.

I do not judge or attack it because it is

the perfect body for me today.

I choose to see it with kindness and compassion.

I choose to bless it instead of cursing it.

The kinder I am to my body,

the more healthy and strong it becomes.

I love and appreciate my body today.

P O W E R   T H O U G H T   # 92

I am learning to make good decisions for myself.

I do not just go along with the crowd and

let them make my choices for me.

I am a powerful creator and I create

through the decisions I make.

I do my research, consult my Inner Guidance

and then make the decisions that are right for me.

God leads and guides me when I tune in.

I am becoming better and better at

making the decisions that are right for me.

POWER THOUGHT #93

I rest in God today.

I will not struggle or strive or try to swim upstream.

I step back and let God lead the way as

I relax and breathe, relax and breathe.

I am on a need-to-know basis with Source and

if there is something for me to do, I will be directed.

If there is something for me to stop doing,

I will be told or shown in simple obvious ways.

I TRUST THAT THE UNIVERSE CAN HANDLE WHATEVER

COMES UP.

POWER THOUGHT #94

I will not judge myself today in any way.

I remember that my goal is progress, not perfection.

I do not have to be perfect – no one is.

I do not have to do everything perfectly – no one can.

I do my very best and then let it go.

I do not expect perfection from others either.

My parents, family and friends are doing

the best they can too – and we are all

learning and growing no matter how old or young.

I can examine my mistakes without judging

or criticizing myself – mistakes are part of the process.

I will not judge myself in any way today.

POWER THOUGHT #95

I release anxiety, stress and feeling overwhelmed.

I soothe myself as I do what needs to be done.

I take my focus off the big picture of ALL that

needs to be done and focus on what is right

in front of me at the moment.

I calmly and lovingly say to myself:

"just do one thing, just do one thing, just do one thing"

as I go about doing one thing at a time.

When that part is done, I go on and do the next part.

I breathe in peace and breathe out anxiety as

I just do one thing at a time.

P O W E R   T H O U G H T   # 96

I take time every day to reflect on the things that

I did well that day, and on what went well.

Instead of doing reruns of every bad thing that

I did or that went wrong, I focus on the positive.

I also focus on where those around me did well.

I am never jealous of the skills or talents of others

but instead am inspired and happy that we

all have different things to bring to the table.

There is no one to compare myself too for

each of us is a unique creation of God.

I acknowledge the Source that made me

when I take time to focus on where

I am getting it right and doing well.

POWER THOUGHT #97

I embrace this new day and the miracles it brings.

I am a radiant beam of Light, which attracts friends,

love, success, good health and joy.

I am not afraid to be happy today.

I am not afraid of love.

Love and acknowledgement shine on me

from all directions today.

Wonderful people are drawn to me and

we love to assist each other in truly helpful ways.

Our relationships are mutually beneficial

and filled with creativity and love.

We are co-creating miracles with Source!

I embrace this beautiful new day!

<u>P O W E R   T H O U G H T   # 98</u>

I live in a friendly Universe.

Though the world can be harsh and unkind,

the Universe is my loving helpful Partner,

bringing into my experience whatever I focus on.

Today I choose to focus on what there is to praise,

honor and appreciate about myself and <u>my</u> world.

I open to receive the gifts of the Universe today

as I clear my mind and open my heart.

This is a wonderful day to be me!

POWER THOUGHT #99

I place my future in the hands of God.

Instead of focusing on problems, I focus on God.

There is no need for me to worry or micromanage

because I know that God is on the playing Field

of my life and is coaching me to great joy and success!

Source has my day, my past, my present & future

in Its loving hands and I can relax my mind

knowing that everything always

works out very well for me.

I am a happy grateful and blessed Child of God.

P O W E R T H O U G H T # 100

Whatever I need to know is revealed to me today.

I have all the Help I need to flow joyfully through this day.

My good is only blocked when I give in to fear,

worry, negativity or bitterness.

Therefore I relax and allow Spirit to open all the right

doors and to bring into my experience all the right people,

places and opportunities to work happy miracles.

Wonderful things are going to happen to me today

and I am blessed and a blessing wherever I go.

POWER THOUGHT # 101

I don't waste my time or energy wishing or hoping.

I am not waiting for anyone to save me.

I make DECISIONS and I know the Universe

responds to me when I make a commitment.

I've DECIDED to be happy.

I've decided to succeed in life.

I've decided to believe in myself.

I've decided to pursue my goals.

I've decided to make a positive difference.

I've decided to do the right things.

I've decided to love and respect myself.

I've decided to take responsibility for my life.

I've decided to seek out mentors who

can teach and guide me with integrity.

I've decided I will save myself.

P O W E R T H O U G H T # 102

I am valuable and worthy because I exist.

My life has meaning and I matter.

No one can do what I came to do or

take my place in the eternal scheme of things.

As I believe in myself more and more,

I know there is nothing I cannot be, do or have in life.

As I believe in myself, I attract others who believe in me.

I am not arrogant, conceited or superior –

I simply remember I was created by God to shine

as brightly as I can, just like everyone else.

I am valuable and worthy because I exist.

POWER THOUGHT #103

God is with me now. There is a Divine Plan for my life.

I believe in the power of God. I believe in miracles.

I believe in the radical action of God's love here on earth.

There is no opposite to this power.

It flows from God through me now.

God uses my hands, feet and voice today

to do the Divine Will.

What a wonderful day of miracles this is

as I remember that God is with me always!

POWER THOUGHT # 104

As I align myself with the Divine Presence in me,

all good is effortlessly drawn to me today.

I cannot fail to be at the right place at the right time.

There is limitless good – more than enough for everyone.

All fear and negativity are washed clean from me now.

There is no need to worry or rush –

the Universe has perfect timing.

I align myself with my greater good today and

watch as success follows success in my world.

POWER THOUGHT # 105

I don't judge according to appearances.

I know that things are often not what

they seem, or what they look like.

I am learning to look more deeply and to

use my intuition to sense the energies present.

Sometimes the most popular people are the loneliest.

Some people who appear very rich may

be deeply in debt and terrified all the time.

Talk is very cheap and people can make

all kinds of promises, but what matters is

what they actually DO.

I'm learning to take my time and not rush to judge.

I am learning to use my intuition to look and

feel more deeply what is happening in my world.

POWER THOUGHT # 106

There is nothing wrong with being different or unusual.

Life is not a competition and there are no winners or losers.

The challenge is to be myself in a world of conformity.

I've decided to keep finding out who I am and

to be true to that as much as I can.

Source did not create me to be a carbon copy of others.

I am enjoying the process of finding out who I am

and I give everyone else permission to do the same.

I don't call anyone names even in private because

I know they are just learning to express who they are too.

We're all finding our way and

there is no one right way to be.

POWER THOUGHT # 107

I am learning to listen to other people so

that I can get to know and understand them better.

Instead of doing all the talking or being in my

own head trapped by my thoughts,

I relax inside and listen to what others are really

trying to say to me or to the group.

I am learning to quiet the critic in my mind

whether the criticism is about others or myself.

I am learning to listen more deeply

with kindness, patience and understanding.

The more I listen, the more I learn and grow.

<u>P O W E R T H O U G T H # 108</u>

I deserve love and companionship and

I am open and receptive to love today.

The Universe brings all the right people and I together and

I gratefully welcome them into my world.

I dissolve any beliefs in separation or limitation.

There are so many wonderful people in this world and

I am continually aligning with my ideal companions.

We love and accept each other just as we are and just as we

are not – there is no need to earn love or approval.

My heart and mind are open to loving companions today.

POWER THOUGHT #109

I release and dissolve any fear I have about food and eating.

My body is a God-vessel and I lovingly feed it without worry,

fear or obsessing because I am Divinely Guided to make the

right choices for <u>MY</u> body without guilt or shame.

I am finding my own balance all the time and I bless

everything I eat and drink instead of cursing or fearing it.

I do not use food to reward or punish myself.

I eat with joy and peace and my body responds

with radiant health and vital energy.

All is well in my world and I have a healthy,

wholesome relationship with my body

and with food.

P O W E R   T H O U G H T # 110

My family and loved ones are surrounded by the White

Light of Divine Protection – there is nothing to fear.

The entire world is being restored to peace and sanity as we

are being led by God to forgive and release one another

from judgment and attack thoughts.

There is no need for defensiveness or to resist evil.

Since what I resist, persists, so I choose to soften my heart.

There is no evil, only the illusion of separation from God.

Today I choose to look past these illusions to the Light

beyond – to the Spirit within.

As I focus on Light, I INVOKE Light and it comes forth.

As Light dispels darkness, love dispels fear.

Today I remember to be the Light of the world instead of

the critic and judge of it.

I speak my Word to invoke healing, light and peace today.

POWER THOUGHT #111

When I am disturbed by anything I remember that
I don't know what anything, including this situation, means.
But if I am willing to be shown by Spirit how to perceive and
see things differently, I can have a miracle replace my upset.

I now ask Spirit to show me the Truth beyond all upsetting
appearances so that I can be at peace again.
I *choose* peace today instead of obsessing about facts.
I have consulted the Higher Authority and once again
I rest in God and trust my Source to guide me.

POWER THOUGHT #112

There are no limits, only limiting thoughts and beliefs.

It is not up to me to determine how miracles happen,

only to remember that "LOTS CAN HAPPEN" if

I let go of trying to control the situation.

Only God can see all the infinite possibilities for good and

there is no need for me to instruct Infinite Intelligence in

how to work everything out. My part is to align.

There is no limit to what can manifest when I align myself

with the Infinite Power and Presence of the Universe.

Today, instead of trying to figure everything out for myself,

I choose to remember that when I turn to God,

LOTS CAN HAPPEN!

POWER THOUGHT #113

Peace is dissolving all resentment and anger in me now.

Above all else, I want the peace of God.

I let go of being right and of arguing for limitations.

I would rather be happy, than be proven right.

I release all hostages now so that I can be free.

I let go of focusing on errors and wrongs now.

I am shredding my files of evidence against anyone and

everyone, including myself.

Today, I choose to only gather evidence for the good

in people, in the world, and in myself.

POWER THOUGHT #114

I was not dropped off on the planet and forgotten.

I have a Divine Companion Who never leaves my side.

I may spend a lot of time ignoring this Guidance,

but it is still being given every day, all day long.

I am tuning in and listening today for this Guidance.

I know that I am loved and cared for totally by my Source.

Today, I ask for Help and then I LISTEN to the Answers that

come so that we may perform miracles together.

POWER THOUGHT #115

I am an eternal God-created Spirit.

I am not bound by a body or trapped in the physical.

I am limitless Spirit, moving through the physical

with ever-increasing Grace and ease.

Spirit is Who and What I am.

I am Spirit and I am free.

P O W E R   T H O U G H T   #116

Good morning Lord!

What miracles shall we do together today?

I am ready and available to be joyfully used

to bring more Light through to the earth plane.

Line it all up and show me what You would have me do.

Miracle working is the most fun there is and

I am eager to get started with today's list!

I will not decide who should be helped or how.

I leave all of that to You as I am on a need-to-know basis.

In this, I release all personal responsibility and instead am a

channel for You to operate through

even if I am not aware of it at the time.

I look forward to the joy of

working happy miracles with You today.

POWER THOUGHT #117

I surrender and dissolve all fear and worry

as again I place my future in the hands of God.

God placed within me everything I need

to experience the best that Life has to offer.

When I am afraid, I am simply leaning on my own strength

instead of remembering my Infinite Source.

I now lean on God and release all future fears.

Everything is unfolding for me in perfect Divine Order

and I look forward to reporting on how it all comes together

in delightful and wondrous ways for all concerned.

POWER THOUGHT #118

Of myself I can do nothing, but there is a Presence within

me that can do ALL things through me.

I now turn to that Presence to lead and Guide me today

so that wonderful things can be accomplished with ease.

I will not judge what occurs because

I trust the Divine Process is working everything out

in perfect timing and miraculous ways.

I get my small self out of the way now to let

my True Self come shining through.

It is another day of miracles and Light!

POWER THOUGHT #119

There is nothing incurable, nothing to be feared.

In God, nothing is so broken that it cannot be restored.

No human "facts" can stop a miracle from happening.

I choose to usher in miracles today and to go beyond facts.

I will not get drawn up in the drama of the

"soap opera of the body" – not my own or

those of other people.

Today, I am ushering in miracles.

POWER THOUGHT #120

Everything always works out very well for me
in perfect ideal timing and ways.
It may not always look like it at first, so I remember to not
judge according to temporary appearances.
Instead, I reaffirm my knowledge that behind every
appearance of limitation is an unborn miracle waiting to
come into manifestation in my world.
I INVOKE miracles by remembering that I am not alone, and
everything always works out very well for me
because I AM a Child of God.

Today, everything is working out very well for me.

POWER THOUGHT #121

Nothing and no one can steal my joy today!

I will not let myself be pulled away from

the center of JOY that God placed in me

when I was created.

I can let things roll off my back today

as I keep coming back to my internal joy.

If something disturbing happens,

I will say to myself,

"NO! I am not going to let that

steal my joy today. I am letting

everyone off the hook so that

I can have a day of inner peace and joy."

POWER THOUGHT #122

I stay in my own yard and weed my own garden.

I was not sent to police the Universe or to live

under the curse of "compare and despair."

What others are doing is not my business —

that is between them and their own Guidance.

I release all hostages today as I focus on the

glory of my own garden and what I choose to

plant and grow for myself.

I am not trying to be busy but only to be fruitful.

I bear good fruit in my life by keeping

my eyes on my own yard and cultivating

my own talents, gifts and abilities.

POWER THOUGHT #123

The only thing that's really true right in this moment is,
"person reading book." Everything else is just a story in
my head – a story I enjoy or dread.
I can change it to a better story, or I can choose
to drop any story in this moment and simply return
to the peace of God by quieting my mind altogether.
I rule my mind, which I alone must rule,
but I can also ask Spirit to exchange my thoughts
for the thoughts of God so that I can return to sanity
and the peace and joy that pass all human understanding.

POWER THOUGHT #124

I am conscious of the energy I bring into
every space that I enter today.
I respect myself and so I respect the
other people around me even if
they are strangers to me.
I don't think only of myself,
but also of the affect I am having on
other people around me through
my behavior and attitudes.
I choose to bring positive respectful
energy into every space I enter today.
I treat others with love and respect
because I treat myself with love and respect.

<u>P O W E R   T H O U G H T   #125</u>

I am responsible for my actions and attitudes.

I cannot blame others for what I do

or for how I feel or think.

And because I am responsible for myself,

I have tremendous power and am

not a victim of anything that has happened in my life.

I am not what has happened to me.

I am not what others have said or done to me.

I am who I choose to be in any given moment.

I am valuable and worthy no matter

what has happened in my life.

I matter and I take responsibility

for remembering that I am a

powerful worthy person.

And because I remember that,

I act like it.

<u>P O W E R   T H O U G H T   #126</u>

I appreciate diversity and contrast in helping me choose.

Living in this diverse world culture I see diversity – things

that I would choose for myself and things I would not.

I am not here to offer endless feedback and

opinions on what I would not want for myself.

The basis of this physical world is free will

and we all get to choose for ourselves.

There is no need to protest unwanted or even to give it

thought as long as I am making my own free choices.

Today I am choosing what I want for myself while

releasing all others to do the same.

I do not need to defend against what others are doing

because God is my refuge and security.

POWER THOUGHT #127

I choose to think gentle loving thoughts today.

I will not give in to attack thoughts against myself,

others, the culture or anything I see or think of

because I know my thoughts do not leave my own mind.

I want a mind that is a wonderful place to rest in so

I am choosing to turn away from attack thoughts

and turn toward thoughts of love, peace, joy & wholeness.

My mind is a wonderful place to be today.

POWER THOUGHT #128

The values of the world are not my values.

The world is always judging according to appearances

and this has made millions of people miserable.

I choose to be joyous and peaceful today by

listening to the still small Voice of God within me

guiding me to see beyond appearances.

I value love, kindness, friendship, family,

generosity, helpfulness, and

mutual support and encouragement.

I am attracting to me the people and experiences

that match my value system and

I know that my path is one of love and joy.

POWER THOUGHT #129

If I feel trapped in some mental story I have the power

to stop the story by simply thinking or saying to myself,

"THE END."

I am not a victim of my own mind or of

any stressful story that I am weaving there.

I am the storyteller and I am free to end it.

I may have to do it 100 times in one day,

but each time I will return to peace and

the remembrance that all things are held

perfectly in the hands of God.

I am the storyteller and I choose to

tell stories of happily ever after today.

POWER THOUGHT #130

No one and nothing has the power to
make me feel bad about myself.
I am still learning and growing every day
and I know that I have a lot to learn in this life.
When those in charge correct me,
I listen with an open heart and mind in
order to do better, but it does not
make me feel bad about who I am.
Everyone makes mistakes, and I know
that I will continue to make mistakes
and learn from them – but I am not a mistake.
There is a difference between my "who" and my "do."
I am a God-created "who" and am therefore worthy.
What I "do" is imperfect and I will always be
learning how to do better as I grow all through my life.
I can love and feel good about who I am,
while still learning how to do better at
this thing called life.
I feel good about who I am.

POWER THOUGHT #131

I don't have to "sell" myself to people.

It's not possible to earn love or approval.

People love who they love and

there's nothing I can do about it.

However, I can be myself today and

draw to me those who love me

just the way I am, and just the way I am not.

I am not auditioning for the world.

I got the part of me and

I am playing it beautifully.

POWER THOUGHT # 132

I cannot out give God but it's fun to try.

Every time I give, more good comes rushing

back to me because of the law of sowing and reaping.

The cost of giving is receiving.

What I put out into the world comes

back to me blessed and multiplied.

Today, I will play the fun game of

trying to out give the Universe as

I share my good with those around me.

The more I give, the more I receive.

POWER THOUGHT #133

I am always at the right place at the right time.

The Universe knows where to find me and

I am never separate or apart from my Source.

Whatever I need is right here, right now,

or quickly on the way to me.

Great things just fall into my lap because

I am always at the right place, at the right time.

POWER THOUGHT #134

I am not here to get the love or approval of others.

God made me and I am sufficient and unique as I am.

I am not broken or wounded and I don't need fixing.

I am lovable simply because I exist as a God-creation.

There is no need to audition for anyone.

Love and approval are already mine.

If I <u>need</u> to change, God will change me.

If I need to be healed, I let God heal me now.

I am not a project. I am a Child of God.

POWER THOUGHT #135

My life is happening here in my own yard.

When I start to give my attention to looking

over the fence and judging what others are doing

or comparing myself with them, I suffer.

My joy and peace come from tending my own garden.

Today, I live and let live as I focus on

doing my best in my own yard –

showing up, prepared, on time,

doing what I said I would do,

with a good attitude.

All the rest is out of my control.

POWER THOUGHT #136

I focus on the beautiful, true and holy today.

My mind is a very holy place and so I fill it with

the most beautiful thoughts and treasures today.

I honor my Divine Mind by not treating it like

a garbage dump for the culture to fill with trash.

I select and cultivate a beautiful mind today

by focusing on whatever beauty I can find.

My mind is a beautiful place to be.

<u>POWER THOUGHT #137</u>

There is no such thing as a small improvement.

Every improvement and step forward is a big deal.

Penguins cross the Antarctic one "tiny" step at a time.

I do not have to overwhelm myself with the

whole big picture or fantasies of perfectionism.

I can take one penguin step forward, then another,

then another, and another.

It is not a race.

What matters is that I am going in the right direction.

I am not counting my mistakes or failures.

I am counting my improvement and steps forward.

I am making wonderful progress today.

POWER THOUGHTS #138

Nothing is cheaper than talk.

I back up my words with positive actions.

I don't just tell people I love them –

I show them with my loving actions.

I don't just say I love myself,

I treat myself with loving-kindness

and take good care of myself.

If someone says they love me,

I don't just take them at their word,

I watch what they do.

Love is not merely and affectionate feeling,

it is a positive consistent loving action.

Today I am backing up my words with action.

I am keeping my promises to myself and others.

I say what I mean, and mean what I say.

POWER THOUGHT #139

I will not argue for my limitations today.

I am a limitless Child of God and all things are possible

when I align myself with the Divine Presence.

Rather than caving in to limiting facts and beliefs,

I consult the Higher Authority and rise up!

Miracles are happening through and for me every day

as I let go of arguing for my perceived limitations.

No one is stopping me from living my dreams

except a silly limiting fearful story in my head.

I am going for my dreams and using my thoughts

to encourage myself to keep going with patience,

persistence and love.

POWER THOUGHT #140

The greatest success in life is to enjoy the journey.

I am not here to fulfill the expectations of others

or of the world around me.

I came to this planet to express Spirit as me.

No one can take my place and denying myself

my joy will not serve the world in any way.

The world is healed by joyful people who

are doing what they love without harming others.

I am one of those people.

I allow myself to enjoy the journey of life

by doing the things that bring me joy.

POWER THOUGHT #141

I can always find something to be joyful about.

My appreciation and gratitude makes me feel

joyful and that joy attracts more to be joyful about.

It is a circle of miracles in which

the better it gets, the better it gets.

I'm interested in seeing just how

great I can let my life get today.

POWER THOUGHT #142

I will return to stillness frequently today.

I know that love is often very quiet and communicates

mostly through actions, while fear talks its fool head off.

Therefore, I will return to the inner quietness today

in order to touch the love that God placed there.

I will listen for the still small Voice instead of to

the chattering voice of fear.

Love speaks to me all through the day and

I am tuning in to hear and respond.

POWER THOUGHT #143

I have a wonderful body,

I love more every day.

It self heals and renews,

In an effortless way.

I have a wonderful body,

I love more every day.

It self heals and renews,

In an effortless way.

I have a wonderful body,

I love more every day.

It self heals and renews,

In an effortless way.

POWER THOUGHT #144

I am taking the positive approach to life today.

It is easy to fall into the temptation of playing

"ain't it awful" with other people in conversation,

but I will not curse my future that way.

I know that every word I speak is prophesying my future

and I choose to speak words of blessing and praise

that sow seeds of success into my present and future today.

I am taking the positive approach to life today.

POWER THOUGHT #145

Since I know that my thoughts never leave my own mind,

I dissolve all fear and attack thoughts with mercy today.

<u>I am the one who suffers from my attack thoughts</u> even

if *"they started it"* or I think they deserve my attack.

I will not justify my attack thoughts because keeping them

only makes me suffer longer as I marinate in them.

I choose mercy and gentleness today for myself and

all those who I think of or see, no matter how much

it seems I am justified in becoming defensive.

I choose to let God handle "them" for me instead

of trying to police the Universe.

I now know that there is no such thing as

a "spiritual warrior."

NO war is spiritual.

Only a peacemaker can bring peace.

I choose to be a peacemaker today.

<u>P O W E R   T H O U G H T   # 146</u>

There is much more good in this world than bad.

We are all more alike than we are unalike.

The news only shows what is unloving

but there is an overwhelming amount of loving,

caring, wonderful people and experiences all around me.

I have decided to seek out and find the good now.

I am like a detective finding clues for the beauty and

wonder in people and in world events.

Right now, heroines and heroes are saving lives

and making the world a safer place to live in.

I am determined to seek and find the good today.

POWER THOUGHT #147

What others think of me is none of my business.

I am an eternal Spiritual Being – I am not a "brand"

and I am not here to shop for friends, lovers, homes,

customers, or any of the forms of the world culture.

I do not need to get anyone's vote or approval.

I am here to express my Divine Nature and to

fulfill the glorious function God gave me.

What others think of me is none of my business.

I think I am a wonderful and as I grow and learn,

I am becoming more wonderful all the time.

<u>POWER THOUGHT #148</u>

It's okay to rest and take time for myself.

I am not missing out on anything by

stepping away from the noise and flashing lights

for a while so that I can rest my mind and body.

My worth does not come from what I DO.

My worth was set by the One who created me.

I can take time to rest in God and

let myself be filled up again with Divine Love.

It is okay for me to turn off the world and go within.

POWER THOUGHT #149

I am not here to hustle or make stuff happen.

I am here to enjoy the journey of life as

I fulfill the function God gave me.

What could be more fun that being a Light

to a world living in darkness?

The Presence that Guides me goes before me

so that I do not need to struggle or push.

Of myself I can do nothing but interfere,

but the Presence within can do all things.

I step back and let God lead the way as

I allow miracles to happen through me.

<u>POWER THOUGHT #150</u>

I am not my job in life to make others happy.

I am not here to fit the pictures of the society

or the people around me.

I set my own standards and terms for success in life.

I seek the guidance and wisdom of my loved ones

and the experts that have gone before me,

but then I make my own decisions and

follow my own unique path and course in life.

It's not possible for me to make others happy.

We all make ourselves happy or unhappy by

the thoughts we think and the actions we take.

I am here to find my own path to success and joy.

POWER THOUGHT #151

Everything always works out for me in the end.

I can let go of stressing out and worrying about

the future because I know that I have it within me

to handle whatever comes along.

I am not weak, but strong.

I am not limited, but limitless.

I am not helpless, but powerful.

I am not angry, but forgiving.

I am not stupid, but am learning.

Things are working out for me as

I remember that I have a Source

that loves and cares for me.

POWER THOUGHT #152

Nothing can harm me today.

Every hand that touches me is a healing hand

and every one I see is another Child of God.

I walk safely and happily through life today

as a grateful open-hearted Child of God.

POWER THOUGHT #153

I have a wonderful future before me.

It doesn't matter where I come from,

only where I am going.

I am not dependent upon what my parents

can give me or provide for me.

I have a Divine Source within me that is

leading me into the life of my dreams.

I know that as I let my mind be still

I can receive Divine Instruction to

move me lovingly forward toward my goals.

I have a wonderful future ahead of me

and I appreciate the present moment as

I follow my inner Call.

POWER THOUGHT #154

It's not my job to try to get others to understand me.

I am more interested in understanding myself

and those around me.

I am not auditioning for friends, a mate or the world.

I am a wonderful unique creation of the One Source

and some will see it and others won't. It's okay.

I didn't come to the world to get approval.

I came for the joyous expansion of my soul!

I seek to understand, more than to be understood.

As I learn to listen to others with my heart and ears,

I am better able to navigate the seas of life.

I love who I am becoming.

POWER THOUGHT #155

I do not let the dire news of the media determine

how I feel about life because I have consulted

a Higher Infinite Creative Authority.

My Divine Source is more powerful than any

world leader, any worldly situation, any thing.

I am optimistic about life because I am coming

to understand that miracles are happening

all the time, all over the planet.

In fact, there is no reason why I should not

have miracles happening in my life most every day.

I am optimistic and enthusiastic about my world.

POWER THOUGHTS #156

I need only do one thing at a time.

If I get overwhelmed it is only because I am believing

my fear thoughts or some stressful story.

I release rushing around and gently focus on

just doing one thing, then the next, then the next.

I relax and breathe and know that everything

is being organized and choreographed by Source.

God is in control of time and space so I know that

miracles will help me accomplish whatever needs doing.

POWER THOUGHT #157

I am making friends with my mind and my thoughts.

I don't have to believe every thought in my mind.

I can CHOOSE the ones that life me UP instead

of that ones that pull me down.

No one else is thinking in my mind.

I am in charge here and I don't need to control

my thoughts – I can simply massage them

into better and better feeling ideas.

I have a wonderful creative mind and

I am learning how to work with it positively.

I choose happy loving thoughts today.

POWER THOUGHT #158

I am not the image I see in the mirror.

The mirror only reflects a distorted concept of me,

but that is not who or what I am.

I can love my body even if

I don't love my reflection all the time.

This body is a vessel I am using while on earth.

I treat it with respect and kindness

regardless of how it appears in a mirror.

My mirror image is nothing at all –

that is not where I am.

I am an eternal spiritual being.

I let go of thinking I am an image

in a mirror or a photograph.

I don't look for myself in a mirror, a photo,

or in the eyes of whoever is looking at me.

I look down at it and feel my spirit inhabiting

it as a wonderful vessel through which I love,

live and experience life here on earth.

I have a body, but it is not found in a mirror.

<u>POWER THOUGHT #159</u>

I am beautiful because God made me.

There is no value in degrading myself because

that only insults the One Who created me.

I give thanks to God for the chance to be the me

that was created by this Loving Divine Source.

Today I love and appreciate myself as a Divine Creation.

POWER THOUGHT #160

I focus on the Light in others today instead of their faults.

This helps me to focus on my own Light & not my faults.

I can focus my mind in whatever direction I choose.

I can look for the good, or the bad.

I can set my own mood today by choosing my thoughts

and choosing how I will see myself and others.

I don't have to wait and see what happens today

before deciding what mood I am in.

No one has the power to "make me" feel a certain way.

I can always CHOOSE my response to others.

I am learning to manage my moods instead of

letting them take control of me.

I enjoy focusing on the Light in others and in myself

because it lifts my mood and makes for a great day.

POWER THOUGHT #161

No one has the power to make me change

how I feel about myself.

What others think of me is none of my business.

I am not here to get "likes" or the approval of strangers.

As I approve of myself, I naturally attract others

who already approve of me too.

I don't audition for the world or try to earn love.

I choose to feel good about who I am and

I don't allow anyone to change my positive self-image.

I am not perfect, because no one is.

But I like who I am and who I am becoming.

I'm pretty cool and I am enjoying being me

more all the time.

POWER THOUGHT #162

People come into my life for a Divine Purpose,

whether they are there for a lifetime or five minutes.

I no longer try to make them stay, or get them to leave.

Instead, I focus simply on accepting that every person

is here so that I can give and receive the blessings of God.

I do not assign to them roles that I think they should fill.

I have no idea the role anyone else should be playing.

Instead, I lovingly open my heart to let the role be

revealed in perfect timing and way by the One Who knows.

What a wonderful Divine Play we are all discovering

in each moment of every day.

I am happy and open to see how it all unfolds today!

POWER THOUGHT #163

Today I am in alignment with God's perfect Will for me.

I know that God's will is my happiness and that

my inheritance is the peace that passes all understanding.

Therefore, I relax my way into alignment with the

perfect plan for a day of limitless miracles and light.

POWER THOUGHT #164

I have feelings, but I am not my feelings.

Feelings are not facts.

They are not good or bad, they just are.

I don't have to judge them or think I "should" feel

a way that I do not feel.

But as I learn to accept my feelings and work with them,

I find that I am not "stuck" in feeling a certain way.

I can grow, and change, and soothe myself into

better feelings by choosing a thought with

a little more breathing space.

It's okay to feel however I feel.

If I do not like the way I feel, I can share those

feelings with a loving person who will listen,

or write them all down

in my journal or notebook, and offer then

to my Divine Source, asking for help.

Feelings are not permanent, they are like the weather

or the clouds passing overhead.

They come and go.

I can savor the ones that feel good, and

ask for wisdom and help with the ones that don't.

POWER THOUGHT #165

I did not come to fix a broken world or to change anyone.

I am here on a Divine Mission to let love come through me.

It is none of my business who receives it or rejects it.

Just as a Lighthouse does not jump off the cliff to

stop a boat from crashing against the rocks,

I do not have to run around trying to save anyone.

My function as the Light of the world is to SHINE

like a Lighthouse or a city set on a hill.

As I shine, people are able to save themselves

by seeing their own Light reflecting back to them.

POWER THOUGHT #166

I ask for help whenever I need it.

I don't hint, or wish people would read my mind.

It is not weak to need or ask for help.

People LOVE to help other people and

if I ask, I can receive.

If I don't ask, I don't get.

The people in life who win the most are

usually the ones who ask for help the most.

I can be strong and independent and confident

and still need and ask for help.

I can be vulnerable and open and hurting,

and ask for help with no shame at all.

Asking for help is a smart thing to do.

And having been helped makes me want

to do the same for others.

We all need help and it is as

blessed to give it as to receive it.

I ask for help when I need it.

POWER THOUGHT #167

It's okay for me to say that I don't know.

I don't have to have all the answers or pretend

that I've got everything figured out or under control.

Smart people ask questions without feeling stupid.

The way to find out and learn is to ask questions.

When I don't know, I say so, and I seek out the answers.

I am smart and I admit when I don't know something

so that I can find out by asking questions.

There are no stupid questions,

only lazy or fearful questioners who won't ask.

I don't have to try to "look good" by faking it.

I am not afraid of what others will think when I ask.

Life is a continual learning curve and

that is what makes it a fun adventure!

POWER THOUGHT #168

I take time to notice the world around me today.

Technology is wonderful but there are also

flowers, and trees, and sky and people all

around to savor and enjoy when I look UP

from a flashing screen or phone.

I am learning to let go of the addiction

to having something in my hand to look at.

I want to experience the freedom and joy

and PEACE that comes from breathing in

the sights and sounds and smells of the

world around me when I look up to nature.

As I look up, my thoughts can slow down

and the stress can drain out of me like

dry sand running through me fingers.

The longer I can put my phone away

the more peace and love I experience in my now.

POWER THOUGHT #169

My goal is the peace of God.

Miracles are following miracles today.

I can easily see the Light in those around me

because this Light grows brighter in my

awareness every day because of my goal.

My goal is the peace of God.

<u>P O W E R   T H O U G H T   #170</u>

I am making good choices today because Spirit is

guiding my thoughts, words and actions.

There is no need for confusion or ego strategies today

for I have turned my mind over to Spirit to guide.

It is as if I am being gently led down a garden path

to the most beautiful Beings Who are all glad to see me!

My mind is able to relax into open spaciousness as

I let Spirit guide all my choices and actions today.

All is well in me and in my world.

POWER THOUGHT #171

I decide who I am today.

I tell the story of me and the world I choose to create.

My past is over and does not determine the self

I choose to be unless I want it to.

I am free to be whoever I choose in each new moment.

I love the self I am today.

POWER THOUGHT #172

I am letting go of self-doubt

and am learning to respect myself.

My confidence in myself is growing every day now

as I learn to let go of self-criticism and condemnation.

I am a wonderful person.

I am willing to love, respect & accept myself

just as I am, and just as I am not.

The way I treat myself is the way others treat me.

I am treating myself with respect and love

and I draw to me others who do the same.

My confidence is not arrogance or conceit.

I am not better or worse than others.

We are all unique and have something to offer.

I see my gifts, and the gifts of those around me.

It is wonderful learning to love & trust myself more.

POWER THOUGHT #173

Nothing is being denied me except by my own thinking.

This is a limitless and abundant Universe

that is cooperative and friendly to me.

Each day I am writing the script of my story of

living happily ever after.

Today I choose to think limitless beautiful thoughts

and watch them manifest in my world.

<u>P O W E R   T H O U G H T   # 174</u>

My worth is not established by my accomplishments.

I am worthy because God created me that way.

I do not have to earn my space on the earth.

By Grace I am blessed, prospered and healed without

struggle, strain or stressing myself out.

I do my work because it feels good to

accomplish things, not because it proves anything.

I contribute because I want to and because it is fun,

not to appease some mythical being who judges.

My God is loving, generous and endlessly good to me.

I contribute to the world out of gratitude to God,

not out of obligation or fear.

POWER THOUGHT #175

I silently bless everyone I see or think of today.

I am a powerful Child of God and I lovingly use

that power today to extend love and peace to humanity.

I know that when I extend blessings, I FEEL blessed too.

As I bless others, my own blessings multiply without limit.

POWER THOUGHT #176

No one is in charge of my happiness except me.
I can choose happiness by directing my thoughts
to appreciation, gratitude and making the best of things,
instead of making the worst of things.
I let go of judging and condemning.
I let go of fear and worry.
It is not selfish to make myself happy by
doing the things I love to do.
When I am happy, I can inspire happiness in others,
but it is not my job to make them happy.
We are all responsible for our own happiness.
When I am sad, angry or afraid, I know that
those are temporary feelings and they will pass
like the clouds pass on a windy day.
I can simply gradually patiently start shifting to
thoughts with just a little breathing space.
I'm not trying to go from sadness to bliss.
I am simply moving myself up an emotional scale
one thought at a time as I select thoughts
that feel better and better and better.

POWER THOUGHT #177

I make peace with my past so that I can be present

for the good that may come to me today.

I cannot "fix" my past, but I can learn from it

how to be more loving, kind and conscious.

My mistakes provide an opportunity for me

to learn and grow in wisdom and love.

I know that love is the most important thing in my world.

As I forgive myself for my mistakes and learn from them,

my love grows and I will do better next time.

I now choose to forgive myself and to let go of the past.

I am not ashamed of my mistakes.

I am making peace with my past and

doing better as I learn and grow.

<u>POWER THOUGHT #178</u>

I do not compare myself with others.

I can be inspired by others, but there is no value

in comparing myself with anyone else.

I will not "compare and despair" today because

I know that we are all unique beings.

My path is my path and is specific to me.

Everyone in my family, school and community is

a unique creation of the Divine Source and

we all have our own role to play in this life.

I am interested in discovering my role instead

of looking to see what everyone else is doing.

I am celebrating my own unique path as

I continue to discover it with each passing day.

I am finding out that I am a wonderful person

with many gifts to contribute in my own way.

I keep focused on my own paper,

in my own yard, in my own lane.

There is no one to compare myself with

because no one came to be me.

I got the part!

POWER THOUGHT #179

I can always calm myself down.

I remember to stop and breathe frequently

when I find myself feeling like my plate is too full

of things to do and remember and such.

I let my shoulders relax, close my eyes for

an instant and let Spirit line everything up for me.

I stay present instead of getting lost in the big picture.

I do not have to belief in the myth of perfectionism.

I am under Grace and am guided and Helped in all I do.

I breathe in the peace of God and breathe out stress.

My body is relaxing in the perfect peace of God

and everything unfolds in perfect timing and ways.

There is plenty of time and plenty of help if

I will just surrender it all to Him.

Today, I am not overwhelmed.

I am perfectly whelmed.

<u>P O W E R   T H O U G H T   # 180</u>

What others think of me is none of my business.

I am remembering this more and more

and it gives me the freedom to be fully myself.

Life is not a popularity contest and

I did not come to get the approval of the world.

I came to find my own joy and to express love.

No one can do just what I came here to do.

I do not need the permission of my peers to

express myself and be who I am.

The more I am myself, the more joy I feel.

I approve of myself and that is all that matters.

In this expansive Universe, I will attract to me

those who are also being themselves.

I do not judge myself, so I do not judge others.

Variety and diversity are wonderful and are

the way the Great Creator made everything.

Sameness and conformity is not nature's way.

I am giving myself permission to be who I am

without worrying what others are thinking.

I am not the thought police.

I am a radiant Child of God.

POWER THOUGHT #181

I have an internal Guidance System which

does not fail me when I consult It.

The world and the media do not have

my best interests at heart, but my Cosmic GPS does.

This GPS is what all the great scientists, inventors,

poets, artists and great thinkers have used

to discover, create and heal.

It is available to everyone but it requires that

I take time each day to tune out the world

and technology so I can go inside and

seek Universal Wisdom and Guidance.

I am learning to turn within daily for

guidance, wisdom and direction

which always leads me in a loving direction.

POWER THOUGHT #182

I focus on savoring the present moments today.

Right now there is nothing for me to do or fix or change.

I am simply opening up to receive Guidance from Source.

There is nothing to grab hold of,

nothing to push away.

I am gently opening to receive.

Now, I will be still and listen to the Truth

as the still small Voice speaks to me of love.

I tune in and receive the word of God today.

POWER THOUGHT #183

There is wisdom in my body and

I am learning to listen to what it tells me.

Instead of mindlessly treating my body with

unkind thoughts and actions,

I am becoming more mindful and tuned-in

so that I can give it what is loving and nourishing.

Source created this body and I will not

judge or attack it today with criticism or judgments.

I do not compare it with other bodies

or expect it to fit any media stereotypes of

what a body "should" look like or be.

I listen to my body and treat it with kindness.

I love and appreciate my beautiful body.

POWER THOUGHT #184

I am filled with gratitude today as
I focus my attention on the beauty of my world.
I am not a critic or judge today because I am
opening my eyes to see how good I have it.
I focus on the positive aspects of my world
and speak words of praise and gratitude
throughout this day.
I give genuine compliments and kind words
to those I come in contact with today.
This is a day of gratitude and appreciation
and since my thoughts never leave my own mind
I know that what I give, I receive.

POWER THOUGHT #185

I am aligning with the prosperous Universe today!

I deserve to be happy.

I deserve to prosper.

I deserve to succeed in life.

I deserve to live.

Therefore, I am accepting the good news that

I am have limitless resources with my reach

as I align myself with the Divine Source.

There is nothing and no one stopping me

but a limiting belief in scarcity or struggle.

I now release all such thoughts and remember

that the Spiritual Truth is Abundant Living!

POWER THOUGHT #186

I am a wonderful person and my heart is full of love.
I know that I have a lot to offer and that I am aligning
with wonderful companions with whom I can share
loving and mutually beneficial relationships.
I release and dissolve any old patterns in relationship
that do not serve me in having joyous
loving people in my life.
I am washed clean of the past by a Divine Grace
which restores me now to joy, sanity and inner peace.
I am a beautiful beam of Light, drawing to me
those who are ready to love, laugh, enjoy
and share this journey through life.
My heart is open to give and receive great love today.

POWER THOUGHT #187

I am a unique creation of the One Divine Mind.

There is no one just like me, no one to compare

myself with and no competition of any kind.

I love and approve of myself today as

a perfect creation of God.

I am not broken, damaged or wounded because

I was created as a self-healing and renewing Being of Light.

I accept myself just as I am, and just as I am not.

If I need to be changed in any way,

Spirit knows how to bring it about it miraculous ways

and in perfect timing.

I accept myself as a Divine Creation of God today.

POWER THOUGHT #188

I ask for and receive the Help of God today.

I am not alone for God is with me now

and I am walking in Divine Light and Love.

Whatever I need to know is revealed to me and

everything always works out well for me as

I cast my burdens on the Christ within me.

I am anointed and I have a joyous function

and all the Help I need to fulfill it with ease.

I have asked God to heal my mind of

all fear, judgment and attack thoughts so

that I may walk in Love and Grace today.

What a wonderful day to be me!

POWER THOUGHT #189

I now dissolve and release all that is no longer

a part of the Divine Plan for my life.

I now open and relax into the greater good which

IS now a part of the Divine Plan for my life.

This is a day of Divine Harvest as I let go

of the old and open to receive the new.

I am excited to see how Spirit works everything

out for the highest good of all concerned today.

I am a vessel for bringing miracles through

as I step back and let Spirit lead the way.

POWER THOUGHT #190

The peace of God is guiding me now.

Wonderful doors are opening for me as

I let go of any need to argue, fight or have the last word.

I prefer the peace of God to being right about my judgments

because I trust the Higher Authority to set all things right.

Love does not win because it does not compete.

Love is not at war with anything or anyone.

Love simply abides, and it abides in me now.

POWER THOUGHT #191

I am doing a fabulous job at life because

I am under Divine Instruction every day.

There is no reason to ever compare myself with

another person or with the culture around me.

I have no category and no competition.

I am a Divine Creation, doing a wonderful job

of being the wonderful Self that God made.

I am unique and no one can take my place.

Today, I savor and enjoy my life as a

unique Creation of the One Source!

POWER THOUGHT #192

I did not come to earth to fix a broken world.

I did not come to fall into line with the culture around me.

I came to express joy and love creatively.

I am a deliberate creator, learning as I go

how to create the life that is best for me.

As I mature, I am learning from my mistakes

and from my successes how to manifest my dreams.

The greatest gift I can give the world is to be

a happy peaceful loving being

and I am in the process of doing just that.

POWER THOUGHT #193

No one can steal anything from me because

all that I have belongs to Source anyhow.

I trust that I am always being taken care of,

so no one can betray or take advantage of me.

There is more than enough good to go around

and anything I lose is restored and increased

by a Law of Divine Compensation.

This means if I am cheated by anyone,

the Source compensates me with something better.

There is nothing I own, for I am only a caretaker

of material things, so there is nothing to fear.

Everything belongs to Source and goes back to Source.

Earth is a glorious temp job and I am simply using

whatever is most useful for my time here.

I am safe and all is well.

<u>P O W E R   T H O U G H T   #194</u>

I am surrounded by love and appreciation all the time

because I love and appreciate myself.

The world only mirrors my own opinions and beliefs and

since I know myself to be valuable, lovable and worthy,

that is reflected back to me everywhere I go.

I respect and value myself. I know my worth.

Love and appreciation come to me daily as

I love and appreciate myself.

POWER THOUGHT #195

I stay in my own yard and tend my own garden.

What others are doing has nothing to do with me.

I have no interest in gossip or comparing myself to others.

I am free and they are free – we are all choosing.

What others choose to do in their garden is their business.

I am so delighted by the seeds I am sowing and reaping

that I have no time to spy on others anymore.

My life is a wonderful garden of delights and

I am pulling out the weeds of worry and fear

as I bear the fruits of love, kindness, peace and joy.

My garden is thriving with good fruit today!

POWER THOUGHT #196

Whatever I have the ability to imagine, I can receive.

The Universe has the resources to guide me in

all the right directions and to match me up with the

right people, in the right places, at the right time.

My job is to BELIEVE in my dreams and to

keep moving in their direction with joy.

My parents are not the source of my good –

my good comes from God, the Universal Source.

God does not give or withhold anything.

Everything comes through vibrational matching.

If my vibe is one that matches my dreams,

then they manifest in my world.

The only exception is if my desire interferes

with the free will or choice of another person.

I cannot interfere or control another person so

I release everyone to create their own dreams too.

Today I am believing my dreams into reality.

POWER THOUGHT #197

I can always turn around when I find myself

feeling separate, angry or afraid.

I am not at the effect of my moods or thoughts.

I can deliberately change my mind and

choose better-feeling thoughts.

I can turn a downward spiral into an

upward spiral by taking some time to

breathe, relax my body, and then

choose how I WANT to feel again.

It takes practice and patience,

but I am learning how to guide my own mind.

I celebrate every tiny step forward.

It is about progress, not perfection.

I can turn around when I am going

in the wrong direction without blame,

guilt or shame.

I am learning.

<u>P O W E R   T H O U G H T   # 198</u>

I am happy in my present moment.

I am not waiting for something to happen before

I start enjoying my life and my world.

Right now I can look around and find things

to appreciate and be happy about.

There are so many blessings in my world already

and I choose to focus on what I have instead

of giving my power and attention to what is missing.

I am happy and grateful in my present moment.

POWER THOUGHT #199

There is nothing inappropriate about me.

There is nothing wrong with me and I am not broken.

Everyone has their own unique set of problems and

challenges to deal with and to find their way through.

Mine are no better or worse than anyone else's.

I cannot judge the path of another just by looking

at their life or what they show to the world.

No one can judge my path either – not even me.

I came here to discover how to create my own

wonderful life through my attention and intention.

Whatever obstacles seem to be in my way are

only helping me to become a more skilled creator.

I CAN live the life I choose if I simply keep

moving forward, even if it is with the tiniest steps.

There is no race. I believe in myself more every day

and I know that my challenges may inspire others

who come after me to know that they can do it too.

POWER THOUGHT #200

I refuse to live my life in fear of the future.

Instead, I place my future in the hands of God

and align with miraculous wonderful happenings.

I do not let the news or government terrify me,

because I have consulted a Higher Authority.

I am believing in the Grace of God to direct me

on what to do, where to go, what to say,

and to whom, every day.

I am learning to see myself as a powerful

miracle worker here on earth,

joyously spreading Light instead of fearing the dark.

POWER THOUGHT #201

God loves me totally, right now, just the way I am.

God loves me totally, right now, just the way I am.

God loves me totally, right now, just the way I am.

God loves me totally, right now, just the way I am.

God loves me totally, right now, just the way I a.

I am enough.

I matter.

My life is important.

POWER THOUGHT #202

I am not a victim of the world around me.

I am a powerful creator and what I have now

does not determine what I can create today and tomorrow.

There are no limits on me except those I believe in.

I choose to see myself as a limitless being with

the potential to create the life I choose for myself.

Source created me as an extension of Itself and

so I have the same capability to be a creator.

I choose to create from love and inspiration.

I do not expect other people or the world to

make me happy or to create for me.

I love creating a life that brings me joy

as I take responsibility for focusing on

gratitude and appreciation instead of dissatisfaction.

I am creating a life I love to live.

POWER THOUGHT #203

Nothing good is withheld from me

and no one is stopping me from happily thriving.

I have an Invisible Supply, which flows forth from

the Kingdom within me.

I do not seek in the external to get my needs met.

My supply is within me waiting to be released by my word.

I release it now to manifest in my world and to bless

all those who come in contact with me or think of me.

I am the rich Child of a Loving Mother-Father God.

There is nothing good withheld from me.

POWER THOUGHT #204

When something disturbing happens,

I do not waste my time and energy on trying to

figure out why it happened or whose fault it was.

Instead, I ask myself "what will I make of this?"

knowing that I can make the worst of it,

or the best of it.

I know that I can either use it as a reason to

close my heart and withdraw into fear,

or as a reason to soften my heart and

become a more loving person in the world.

I cannot control what happens in the world,

but I can decide how I will respond to it.

POWER THOUGHT #205

When I am joyously creating,

I am contributing to the whole Universe.

I allow myself to dream big and to keep

expanding my mind to know that

nothing is impossible with God.

There is no order of difficulty in God.

One miracle is not bigger or harder than another.

They are all equal to my Source.

I am not going to keep myself small

because I have a big generous loving God

who loves me beyond the beyond.

POWER THOUGHT # 206

I cannot make others happy by joining them in misery.

Sitting and complaining does not make things better.

I can listen with compassion to others without

joining them in limited thinking or in suffering.

I do not have to fix their problems or give them

the perfect advice or answer.

I can listen with kindness and patience

and simply ask, *"Is there anything I can do?"*

I do not judge them or wish they were different.

I send them love and know that they also have

the same Infinite Source I do, even if they don't know it.

The way I pray for them is by imagining them happy,

peaceful, prosperous, healthy, loved and loving.

POWER THOUGHT #207

I know my parents/guardians are doing the best they can.

I may not agree with everything they think and believe,

but I know that we are on the same team and

I am grateful to them for giving me life.

We are who we are, and it's okay if we do

not always understand each other.

I show them I love them as often as possible.

I thank them for the things they do for me.

I do what I can to help around our home

because I appreciate having a place to live.

I do not take them for granted.

I do my best to get along with everyone in our home.

I ask for God's help in seeing my parents with

love, understanding and compassion.

We are all doing the best we can

and with God's help will do better as we grow.

POWER THOUGHT #208

I do not let the culture dictate or dominate my thoughts.

I know that the world culture is rooted in fear, attack

and scarcity thinking, and this is not what I want.

Instead, I choose to listen ONLY to the Divine Voice within

me that reminds me of the beauty and kindness of Life.

Cursing and fearing the darkness is useless, so

I choose to turn up my Light no matter the circumstances.

I am the Light of the world and I treat my mind as a

holy vessel and not as a dumping ground for the media.

I choose to fill my mind with love, peace and Light today.

POWER THOUGHT #209

Wonderful people are drawn to me and we

bring out the very best in each other.

I praise and compliment the people around me

and watch them blossom like flowers in the sun.

We encourage and uplift instead of tearing down.

The more we praise each other, the more there is to praise.

In school, work & play, I attract and bring out the best in

others & this blesses & enriches my world in amazing ways.

I love people, and people love me!

POWER THOUGHT #210

I am not my grades or accomplishments in life.

I am not my body or the family I come from.

I am not my past or my mistakes.

I am a beloved child of the Universe.

I cannot be seen in a mirror, on a report card,

on a weight scale, or on an aptitude test.

I can be seen only with the heart and an open mind.

I am opening my heart and mind to see others today

instead of judging them according to appearances.

I am giving what I want to receive by

seeing others with my heart and clear open mind.

POWER THOUGHT #211

I can always calm myself down.

Whatever is happening, I can go inside, take 3 slow

deep breaths, clear my mind and pull myself back

to a more peaceful place inside.

I don't have to let my thoughts rule me.

I can let my breath clear out the fearful thoughts

and come back to a place of calm inside.

My breath is my friend in staying calm and peaceful.

POWER THOUGHT #212

I cannot control other people or the world around me.

In fact, it is doing harm to myself to even try.

Instead, I can be a positive influence by controlling

my own reactions to people and situations.

I do my best to respond from kindness instead

of reacting from fear or anger –

and the only way I can do that is if

I practice choosing my own thoughts every day.

It is not up to me to control anyone or anything,

but it is my job to gently guide my own thoughts

in a direction that brings me more peace.

If I am peaceful and loving,

I may be a loving peaceful influence on the world.

POWER THOUGHTS #213

I seek first to understand others,

instead of struggling to be understood by them.

If I can truly listen to others, and show them

that I hear what they are saying,

it is more likely that they will then be

willing to listen to me too.

I can listen without being defensive or

trying to fix them.

I can simply listen with kindness and love.

People just want to be heard and seen.

As I grow, I am listening to others

and listening to myself.

This makes my relationships wonderful.

POWER THOUGHT #214

I am making a positive difference in the world

through the love and kindness I am sharing.

I am a loving and generous spirit and I am guided

by God where to give my gifts and when.

I do not give out of sacrifice, but out of the

abundance of the Kingdom within me.

I am giving love and kindness because

I know that I am an abundant being.

I give out of the great treasure of my heart

and it comes back 1,000 fold and more.

POWER THOUGHT #215

I am not competing with anyone else.

There is no better or worse, just different.

I'm learning to appreciate myself and my

unique way of doing things without comparing

myself to anyone else in the world.

God doesn't make junk or mistakes.

What others call "weird" is often a very

unique "limited edition" to be treasured.

<u>P O W E R   T H O U G H T   # 216</u>

I can decide the kind of day I want to have

by choosing how I want to feel.

Unexpected things may happen today,

but I don't have to let that throw me.

I can keep remembering how I want to feel, and

keep coming back to that feeling as much as possible.

As I practice this, I become more stable and can

count on myself to be there for myself even

if seems no one else is.

Today, I have decided I want to feel _____.

POWER THOUGHT #217

My relationships grow more wonderful every day.

I let go of trying to change or fix others –

and of trying to change or fix myself.

I am practicing loving acceptance of us

just as we are, and just as we are not.

I release judging or gossiping about others.

I release judging myself too.

Today, I am focusing on seeing the good

in myself and everyone around me.

This is going to be a wonderful day!

POWER THOUGHT #218

I can do whatever I set my mind to do.
It may take me a long time to learn how and
to gain the knowledge and skills, but if I keep on
moving in the direction of my desire,
I can achieve whatever I set my mind to.
I have patience with myself while I am learning.
I encourage myself every day instead of
getting discouraged when I make a mistake.
Everyone starts somewhere and this
is where I am starting.
It's a very good place to start.
I know that I can do whatever I set my mind to do –
and if I eventually change my mind and no longer desire
to do whatever it is, I am not a failure.
The way to learn is to investigate and make the effort.
I am in the process of finding out who I am!

POWER THOUGHT #219

It's okay if I have an opinion that is unpopular.

Many of the greatest people in history thought

differently than the people and systems around them.

I can feel differently and still respect the opinions of

those around me and listen to them without attack.

And if it is a safe space, I can share my thoughts too.

We don't all have to agree with each other,

but it is wonderful that we can listen to

each other without fighting or attacking.

I am not focusing on having the popular viewpoint

but on coming from a loving place.

It's okay for me to be different

or to think differently.

POWER THOUGHT #220

I am not going to chew on old resentments against

people who have hurt me or upset me

like and old piece of gum I've had too long.

I'm focusing on my present and future

instead of regurgitating old past wounds.

Instead of looking out the rear view mirror,

I am looking at my beautiful journey now

and the road ahead through the windshield.

I'm not doing reruns of old conversations and

stories that hurt or anger me.

I choose to let all that go so that

I can focus on whatever good there

is for me to look at today –

even if it is just a bird, a stream, or

a friend smiling at me.

POWER THOUGHT #221

I notice the abundance of the Universe around me.

There is so much good flowing forth every day –

so many flowers, trees, birds, stars, grains of sand!

This must be an abundant world of plenty

and I am an important part of it.

Therefore, I am being supplied as I open up

to let Source flow through me.

There is so much money floating through the air

and I open to let it flow to me now.

There are limitless opportunities flowing forth

and I open to see and receive them now.

My world is abundant and I am limitless.

POWER THOUGHT #222

I value, respect and am proud of myself.

My life matters. I am important.

I am irreplaceable in the Divine Plan.

I am not better or more important than others.

We are all equal in God.

We are all the multi-colored threads in the

Master Tapestry of life.

Each of us has an important part to play.

Bigger is not better.

Smaller is not less important.

We all matter.

I value, respect and am proud of

my part today.

I value and respect others.

This is a great day to be me.

POWER THOUGHT #223

I am surrounded and filled with Love today.

This love leaves no room for fear or judgment

in my consciousness and it dissolves all limiting beliefs.

I open my heart to this Divine Love like

a flower taking in the radiant morning sun.

I send this love back out as a beacon to

light the way today.

I am a lighthouse of Love today.

POWER THOUGHT #224

Because I respect myself, others respect me.

I know that no one can give to me what

I am not willing to give myself.

Therefore, as I give myself love and respect,

I attract others who reflect that love and respect for me.

I do not lower my standards to fit in.

The way I treat myself is the way others will treat me.

I treat myself with love, respect and kindness

and it sets the standard for how the world treats me.

POWER THOUGHT #225

I am happy in my now and optimistic about my future.

There is great good before me as I continue to

expand my ability to believe in miracles and Grace.

Current economics, trends, political situations and

cultural happenings have nothing to do with me

because I live by Grace and not by the fears of the world.

I expect and accept miraculous unfolding good

today as I step into the Greater Reality

of God's limitless bountiful Grace for me.

I may not like everything that is happening around me,

but I can always find something to appreciate and

be grateful for in my world.

Gratitude and appreciation expands my joy.

I've decided to be joyful today.

POWER THOUGHT #226

My Source is lavish, extravagant and generous.

My Source is the same One that created the grains of sand

on all the beaches, all the stars in the cosmos and

all the leaves on the trees - everything that the eye can see.

How can I be limited with such a glorious Source?

I reach deep within myself today to remember

I am one with my Source, therefore,

I can be who I want to be in this life.

I can do what I want to do in this life.

I can have what I want to have in this life.

I have a limitless, lavish, extravagant, generous Source.

POWER THOUGHT #227

From time to time today, I let my mind relax.

At any moment I can STOP my mind,

close my eyes, take a deep breath, and let go

of everything that has happened so far today.

I can release all the tension in my body and

let it drain away like sand through an hour glass.

I let my shoulders drop, I relax my jaw,

and my belly, I breathe into my heart and let it open up

to receive the love of my Source.

In these moments I let my thoughts slow down

and I let go of what is happening on social media,

in my family, with my friends, and in the world.

I relax my mind and go inside myself to a

Kingdom of inner peace and tranquility for

a few moments while I relax and breathe, relax and breathe.

POWER THOUGHT #228

I am becoming more and more confident

and believing in myself more every day.

I don't focus on my weaknesses and mistakes.

I am amplifying what is right with me

instead of what I think is wrong with me.

I am not arrogant or conceited because I know that

we all have different gifts and talents.

There is something beautiful and wonderful about all of us.

But I am also not playing small or weak out of fear that

others will think I am showing off.

Loving myself is not conceited.

Loving myself honors the Source which created me.

I am just being myself and focusing on bringing

my best to the table.

I don't have to be good at everything.

I am not focused on perfection, but on progress.

I am making progress at my own pace,

and this makes my confidence grow.

I believe in myself no matter what anyone

else thinks or says about me.

I believe in myself and in my future.

POWER THOUGHT #229

I trust my intuition and my gut feelings.

If something doesn't feel "right" to me,

I don't do it just because others want me to.

I don't sell out on myself to please others.

They are not my Source.

I don't go along with things I don't believe in.

I follow my own inner guidance system.

I can say no to what doesn't feel right to me,

even if it means I don't seem "nice" to others.

I am responsible for my actions, not others.

If someone is trying to manipulate me into

doing something that is wrong for me,

that person is not really my friend.

I respect myself too much to sell out on me.

I am learning to trust my intuition and follow it

even when it is uncomfortable in the moment.

This is my ticket to a joyous successful future.

POWER THOUGHT #230

There is only one power and Presence.

There is nothing to oppose God, nothing to battle or fight.

I need not "resist evil" because what I resist will persist.

Instead, I turn away from the darkness and toward Light.

I invoke this Light by activating It within myself.

I no longer see teams, sides, or enemies.

I am focusing on oneness and know that

in that Oneness, all is well.

If I am afraid today, it is because I am believing

in the lie of separation and opposing sides.

I claim my miracle by remembering that

there is only God, God, God –

and I am One with God, now and forevermore.

Right here, right now, even if things are not to my liking,

all things are held perfectly in the hands of God

and I am safe.

POWER THOUGHT #231

I am using my mind constructively and positively.

I don't have to believe everything I think.

I can question my stressful thoughts, turn them around

and release the stressful ones back into the nothingness.

I get to choose what I allow into my mind

and the thoughts I will entertain and make welcome.

Today, I choose the thoughts that feel good

when I think them. I take a positive approach.

I don't have to think the most affirmative positive

thoughts anyone has ever thought.

I can simply reach for a better-feeling thought.

I am taking responsibility today for guiding my

mind to the thoughts that have more breathing space.

POWER THOUGHT #232

Wonderful things are going to happen to me today.

I am opening my mind and heart to see the beauty of life.

Life is blessing us all and I am open to see it today.

I take all the good personally and let the rest go.

Every flower, tree, bird and kindness is a gift from Source.

I choose to give everyone a break today as

I overlook all rudeness, mistakes and ugliness.

I am making the best of things today instead

of getting off track by policing the world.

The more I focus on the wonderful things,

the more wonderful things keep happening for me.

POWER THOUGHT #233

I am approaching life with courage and confidence today.

I have so much to offer and I am letting the world see it!

People love me, and I love people.

I forgive and release the past and am open

to new opportunities, new people, and new life.

Everywhere I go today I am drawn to the

highest and best that Life has to offer.

I see and appreciate Life's beauty as

I move confidently in the direction of my good.

<u>POWER THOUGHT #234</u>

I can be who I want to be,

do what I want to do,

and have what I want to have in life.

No one is stopping me and no one

can limit me but my own beliefs.

I am believing and investing in myself now.

I can be, do and have the life I choose

as I take the steps to achieving my goals.

<u>POWER THOUGHT #235</u>

I am patient as I persevere and go in the direction

of my goals and greater good in life.

I do not let obstacles stop or discourage me.

I know that with Source there is always a way and

so I lean on God instead of leaning on people.

I can rest and regroup when I need to

but I can then carry on and take the next step forward.

I congratulate myself for each step forward

and allow it to inspire me to keep going.

I release the timing and my pictures of how things can

happen to Source to work out in wonderful ways

as I continue to patiently go in the right direction.

I am patient as I persevere in working miracles.

POWER THOUGHT #236

I focus on progress, not perfection.

I do my best and forget the rest.

Perfection is an unobtainable illusion,

but honest effort on my part is possible.

I show up, prepared, on time,

doing what I said I would do to the best of

my ability, with a good attitude and

what happens after that is out of my control.

I acknowledge myself for showing up.

POWER THOUGHT #237

I am enthusiastic about the possibilities of this new day.

I look forward to watching how Spirit works

out all things for my highest good

as I am joyfully used to do God's Will.

I offer my heart, hands and voice today

to be truly helpful to whoever I am guided to help.

I know that we will all be blessed as

I happily give and receive the peace of God today.

POWER THOUGHT #238

No one can take the good that belongs to me.

I am never rejected. I am merely spared.

If a door slams shut in front of me,

it is for my own greater good and

I have been spared from wasting my time or energy.

There is another door that will open for me

In the perfect ways and timing as

I keep my heart and mind open

to the Guidance of Source.

My feelings are not hurt for I believe that

the wisdom of Source is sparing me and

guiding me to a better way to go.

I am guided and gently corrected as I go.

POWER THOUGHT #239

I am worthy of the gifts and Guidance of God.

I am not timid or shy in asking Spirit to help me.

I know that it is God's good pleasure to give me the

Kingdom and I am in alignment to receive it today.

I know that Life is responding to my Consciousness

and I have a Consciousness of receptivity today.

This is the perfect day for dreams to come true.

I do not have to wait for better conditions or appearances

in my world before I can receive my greater good.

I am worthy now, and I am opening to receive now.

It is impossible to earn the gifts of God or

they would be wages and not gifts.

I need only be an open gracious receiver

in order to accept the blessings of God.

I am an open gracious receiver today.

<u>P O W E R   T H O U G H T   # 240</u>

I encourage and cheer myself on today.

I let go of all self-criticism and attack because

I know that is an attack on a Child of God.

I extend kindness, gentleness and mercy on myself today

as I go about my daily comings and goings.

I let go of perfectionism and impatience with myself.

I take note of even my smallest successes instead of

dwelling on or amplifying my mistakes and shortcomings.

I am on my own team today, cheering myself on

as I amplify every bit of good that I can find in myself.

I am building myself up instead of tearing myself down.

I am not better or worse than others.

I am not competing with anyone.

To say I am on my own team means that I am

<u>for</u> activating love in myself instead of fear.

I am cheering myself on today.

POWER THOUGHT #241

I am not here to get the approval of others.

I am here to be myself.

There is no one just like me.

I am an original unique Divine Creation.

I approve of myself and like myself.

It is important for me to like myself

because I am going to be with me forever.

I am learning to be my own best friend

by approving of and liking myself

even when I make mistakes or fail.

I will be learning and growing my entire life

so I look forward to getting to know myself

more with each passing day and year that passes.

I like and approve of myself.

<u>POWER THOUGHT #242</u>

I am a lovable and capable person

with a lot to offer the world.

I do not judge myself my the standards

of the culture around me.

Instead, I focus on how much of

my true self I am expressing each day.

I take time to work, play, rest and

get in touch with my own inner nature.

I am not here to get the approval of others.

I am lovable and capable of attracting to me

the life that will best suit who I am in life.

I trust myself and I trust the process of life.

POWER THOUGHT #243

I am comfortable making decisions and then

taking positive action based on my decision.

The Universal GPS directs me once I have

made a decision about my destination

and I am guided and course-corrected all along the way.

I enjoy making decisions and savoring the journey

once I have decided where I want to go.

There is no rush, no stress.

I always arrive at the perfect time.

POWER THOUGHT #244

This is an abundant Universe.

There is enough good for me and for all others.

We are all capable and responsible for our own good

for we draw from a Limitless Divine Source.

Miracles are given by those who temporarily have more,

to those who temporarily have less.

No one is more connected to Source than another.

I know that all those I choose to help are no less than myself

and I do not pity them or see them as victims.

I help because it feels so good to help and

because I have been helped and will need it again.

We are all inter-dependent and are able to be of use

to the whole through our loving participation in life.

Source is our Source, but Source acts *through* people.

Today, I remember that all have equal access to Source,

and I allow Source to joyfully use me as an avenue

to deliver miracles to those who are open to receive.

POWER THOUGHT #245

I allow others to contribute to me and

I make it easy for them to do so.

I release all false pride and resistance as

I open to receive God's Help *through* other people.

I let go of victim/martyr thinking.

I let go of thinking I have to do everything myself.

If I need help, I ask people specifically for that help and

then I truly release them to say yes or no with no guilt.

I let go of thinking others can read my mind or

thinking they *should* know what I want.

I make it easy for others to contribute to me

instead of making it more difficult.

It is not weakness to ask for help.

It is intelligent and strong to ask for

and receive the loving contributions of others.

I am open and happy to receive today.

<u>P O W E R   T H O U G H T   # 246</u>

I am learning to say no to what does not serve me.

I do not have to get sick to say no or to "get out of"

doing things I do not want to do.

I do not have to make up stories or excuses

for the choices that I make in life.

I release others to do the same with me.

I now release guilt and manipulation from

all my relationships as I give us permission to

tell the truth without attack or defensiveness.

I keep my heart open and I speak from

kindness and love, but with firmness.

I am saying no when I mean no,

and yes when I mean yes.

It feels good to live from my truth.

POWER THOUGHT #247

When I set my mind to something

I know that I am able to accomplish wonderful things.

God gave each of us free will to choose how

we will perceive ourselves, our life, and the world.

I am no longer making excuses about anything.

I am not trying to fit in anywhere.

I let go of trying to please an insane culture.

I no longer go after goals that the culture has set for us

because they either fail or do not bring me peace.

I am setting my mind only on those things that

inspire and uplift me from now on.

I am setting my mind and keeping it set

on the things that I feel passionate about

and I know that when my mind is set,

miracles follow.

POWER THOUGHT #248

I am dropping the blame-game from my life

so that I can play the PRAISE GAME.

Finding fault with the world and people in it

only brings me stress, anger and frustration.

I am now turning my full attention to all the

wonderful Answers, instead of the problems.

I am giving my life energy to taking a positive approach.

The more I feed the positive Answers,

the more the negative problems fade away

from not being fed by my energy.

I am feeding the positive approach in my life

by playing the PRAISE GAME.

I take time to thank and acknowledge anyone

I see making a positive difference.

I encourage and support those who are helping

instead of cursing and blaming those I judge.

I am taking a positive approach to life.

POWER THOUGHT #249

I am learning to like myself more each day.

I do not have to be perfect in order to like myself

or to honor and appreciate myself.

Making mistake is part of human growth process so I let go

of ridiculous perfectionism and self-criticism.

There is nothing wrong with me.

I am a unique person with unique gifts and frailties.

What others think of me is none of my business.

I enjoy my own company and the company of others

because I like myself and I like other people.

It's a great way for me to live.

POWER THOUGHT #250

Every day in every way, I am getting better and better.

And every day in every way, my life gets better and better.

I am so blessed to know these Principles of creation

so that I can choose how to perceive myself and my world.

I let God bless me beyond all past precedent as

I continue to dissolve and release all limiting beliefs.

I let go of any resistance I may have to thriving and

enjoying my life to the fullest.

Every day in every way, I am getting better and better.

POWER THOUGHT #251

I do not believe in a disastrous future.

I do not feed fears of what may happen someday.

I believe in a friendly Universe and in the Power within me

to respond in creative and loving ways to whatever comes.

I am making a positive difference in the world just by being

alive on the Earth at this time.

I trust myself to do the loving thing.

I trust myself to take good care of myself.

I trust my Source to guide me all the days of my life.

I am looking forward to my future and all it will bring.

<u>POWER THOUGHT #252</u>

Magical and wonderful things happen to me

every day, including today.

In my world, there is bountiful good,

enough to share and to spare.

I go forth today knowing that I am

in alignment with the best that Life has to offer.

I expect wonderful things to happen for me today.

POWER THOUGHT #253

I only tell happy stories about myself and my life now.

I have let go of the dead past and am opening

up to the limitless good that Source has for me today.

I dissolve any mental patterns of scarcity or attack

and rest in the abundance and peace of

the Kingdom within me as

I watch it manifest in form before me.

My world is a welcoming and happy place today.

I find it easier and easer to calm and center myself.

I let go of stress easily and quickly now.

I am enjoying training my mind to focus on the good!

<u>POWER THOUGHT #254</u>

I am practicing believing the best for myself.

I know that if I can believe it I can achieve it.

I see myself growing and thriving more every day.

I give myself permission to be my unique self.

I do not gossip or listen to gossip.

Instead, I run my own race and stay in my own lane.

What others are being, doing and having has nothing

to do with me or what I can accomplish in life.

There is no competition because there is enough good to go

around in this limitless creative Universe of expansion.

Every day now, I practice believing the best for myself.

There are no limits on my future.

POWER THOUGHT #255

I can absorb whatever losses come in life.

I know that there is pain, loss and grief in this life but

I also know that there is a Healing Power in me to

help me thrive regardless of any loss or sorrow.

I have the capacity to heal from anything.

I do not have to give in to despair.

I can go at my own perfect healing pace.

There is no rush.

What is important is to keep going forward.

I can take one step forward each day and continue

to grow into all that is for my greater good.

I can gently absorb whatever loss comes in my life.

POWER THOUGHT #256

My tolerance for joy, pleasure and fun is increasing.

There is no limit to how great I can feel and

I release any guilt or inhibitions around enjoying life fully.

There is no such thing as "having too much fun."

I can accomplish many wonderful things even

while I am having fun and enjoying what needs to be done.

I let go of any religious notion that God wants me to

sacrifice or that serving the Light means manifesting

like and ascetic or moving to India unless I love India.

It is God's desire that I be happy and

I share that desire with God.

I am becoming more and more comfortable with

a life of joy, pleasure, peace and fun.

POWER THOUGHT #257

No one needs to acknowledge or understand me but me.

I am not a beggar seeking the approval or understanding

of the people or world around me. That's my job.

As I acknowledge and understand myself,

I am in alignment with those who will reflect that back.

I am not auditioning for life. I already got the part.

I get to be me! This is a wonderful role to play!

I am learning to understand and appreciate myself

and I release the belief that I need others to do it for me.

I am loving playing the part of wonderful, wonderful me!

Today, I am giving myself the understanding and

acknowledgment that I desire.

I have freed the hostages I took when I was mentally

demanding that they approve of me or see me.

It's MY job to see me, MY job to approve of me.

I do that now. I see me. I approve of me.

I release all others to do as they choose

and this sets ME free as well.

POWER THOUGHT #258

Source-in-me is using my hands, feet and voice today to

accomplish the Divine Will with ease.

I have no idea what anyone needs or how to help them.

Instead, Spirit is arranging and choreographing all

the details for the perfect unfolding of miracles.

I realize that the miracle may be saying "no" to someone

or some other action that may seem "unspiritual" to

the ego thought system which judges by appearances.

Therefore, I will not judge according to appearances but

rather assume that Source is in control here and that

everything is unfolding in according with the Divine Will.

I step back and let God-in-me lead the way.

POWER THOUGHT #259

I relax into the state of calm delight today.

I am not attached to outcomes so

I do not freak out when things seem to go wrong

nor get off center with overexcitement when

things seem to go right.

I relax in gratitude and calm delight as

I watch with wonder a day of miracles which

leads me back to my calm joyous center within.

<u>P O W E R   T H O U G H T   # 260</u>

I am learning to accept other people for who they are.

Instead of judging others and thinking they should live by

my rules, I am learning to see that we are all doing the best

we can from the way we see the world.

There is room for many different viewpoints and ideas.

I do not attack the way others choose to live or ask them to

live according to my standards for them.

I see us all through kind eyes of love as best I can.

I am not perfect at this, and that is okay.

I am learning as I go and as I accept others for who they are

it is easier to accept myself for who I am.

POWER THOUGHTS #261

I do not have to take things so seriously.

I have a whole lifetime ahead of me to learn and grow.

Being myself is what is important and I know that my self is

a Divine Creation, which is lovable and important.

I am worthy and lovable because I exist,

not because of what I do or achieve in life.

My goal is to do my best and learn as I go.

It is not my job to please the whole world or to do

everything perfectly so others will feel good.

I can give myself a break

<u>I am</u> giving myself a break.

I'm giving everyone else a break too.

P O W E R   T H O U G H T   # 262

I take time every day to go within and center myself.

After school or work, I sit down and focus on letting go of

the day and any stress or upsets which may have happened.

I close my eyes, take some deep breaths, and let it all go.

There is no value in carrying it around on my shoulders.

I forgive myself and I forgive all others in the process.

It feels good to let go.

It feels good to go inside myself to the quiet place.

It feels good to forgive myself and others.

I choose to let go of past hurts and stresses.

I choose to let go of worry and regret.

I can let go simply by breathing it all out

Deep gentle slow breathing heals me.

POWER THOUGHT #263

I release my family from my expectations

of who I want them to be.

I release them from doing what I want them to do.

I ask for what I want, but I do not demand it.

I understand we are all doing the best we can.

My parents are just human beings.

They do not need me to save them or fix them and it's not

even possible for me to do so.

I can only love and accept them as they are.

As I want to be accepted, I accept others.

I look for the best in my family and focus on

where they are getting it right instead of

where I think they are getting it wrong.

I also focus on where I am getting it right instead of

where I think I am getting it wrong.

It feels good to accept myself and others as we are.

POWER THOUGHT #264

I give love and praise to my loved ones today.

I am making a habit of thanking my family for being there

for me, for the food and the home and for driving me

around and taking care of me.

I do not take them for granted or think they know

how I feel about them without me saying it.

I speak words of sincere appreciation frequently because

I know that it fills our home with a love vibration.

I encourage and uplift others whenever I can because it

feels good to focus on the positive in life.

As I encourage others, I feel encouraged too.

As I speak words of gratitude and appreciation, my heart

fills up with love and joy.

POWER THOUGHT #265

I release the need to be right or to have the last word.

It is not my job to enlighten or correct other people

or the world at large with my "good ideas."

Everyone has equal access to Source so

I let go of trying to save others or to police the Universe.

Instead, I let Source guide me to those whom

It wants to help through me today.

We will find mutual benefit and blessings

as we are healed together by Spirit.

I know that it will happen without tension or fighting.

It will happen in natural wonderful ways and

I release myself from attachment to any outcome.

I place us all in the Hands of God where all is well.

POWER THOUGHT #266

I am comforted by the Holy Spirit.

I know that there are things which are simply too big

for me to handle with only my small human self.

But God-within-me can handle all things and

make all things possible regardless of how big or small.

The Divine Mother-Father within is Love Itself

and when I feel weak or afraid, I can lean

on the everlasting arms to give me strength and peace.

No matter what happens in my world,

I know that I can be comforted by the Holy Spirit

and taken safely through any storm.

POWER THOUGHT #267

Nothing can separate me from the Love & Presence of God.

No matter how many mistakes I make or how many

times I fall down and fail myself or others,

I know that God loves me and can restore me

to peace, joy, sanity and inner peace if

I will simply ask and then allow it to happen.

I choose to let God restore me now and

to guide me in my thoughts, words, actions

and perceptions so that I may be of joyful use.

POWER THOUGHT #268

There is something wonderful for me to do in the world.

I may not have the slightest idea of what it is yet, but I know

that it exists and that in time I will find my right place.

No one can fill the place that it mine in this world.

No one can replace my part in the grand Scheme of Life.

There is someone wonderful for me to be in the world.

I am discovering myself more every day and it is the great

adventure of my life to continue to evolve and grow into

the wonderful being I was created to be.

There is no one in all the world just like me.

I am important and irreplaceable and I have a wonderful

role to play in the joyous expansion of this Universe.

POWER THOUGHT # 269

Money is just another form of energy.

It is not good or bad – it is just an exchange of energy.

It is fun and easy to play the money game.

I can spend, save, give and invest.

I can earn, receive, accept and create

as much money as I want in my life.

My parents are not my source.

I have a growing wealth consciousness and am able to

attract and create money through work, investing, and

through many ways which are honest.

I know that I can create value and that value brings money.

There is nothing good or bad about money

It is fun to play the money game with integrity and to see

how much of it I can grow and use lovingly and joyfully.

<u>P O W E R   T H O U G H T   # 270</u>

My past does not determine my future.

The past of my family and loved ones

does not determine my future.

Where I came from, what has happened to me,

what others have said about me – none of these things are

obstacles to my happy life and success.

I get to determine my own path in life.

The past is over and I have no need to drag it into today.

I forgive and release any negativity of the past and I allow it

to make me a wiser, kinder, more loving person.

I let go of the past and create a wonderful day today.

I choose to focus only on the loving, happy things in my past

and on the lessons I have learned from my mistakes.

I have a wonderful joyous happy future ahead of me.

POWER THOUGHT #271

Knowing what I don't want only has value

in clarifying what I *do* want.

Instead of focusing on what I don't want,

I allow the contrast between wanted and unwanted

to help me focus only on what I *do* want today.

I release the past and focus on the road ahead.

I am the one who sets my destination by

what I choose to focus on and the goal ahead.

Today I am setting my GPS for the goal

that I want as I listen to my intuition

guiding me on my highlighted route

to a happy successful day.

POWER THOUGHT #272

I don't judge my feelings.

My feelings are just feelings and even the most painful ones

can pass like clouds on a windy day if I will can relax and let

my breath bring me back to calm sanity.

I do not have to believe every thought that passes through

my mind or react to every feeling I have in the moment.

I trust myself to heal and I know that feelings are temporary

no matter how intense they are in the moment.

My feelings are not right or wrong – they just are.

I do not have to react to my intense feelings.

I never hurt myself or another person because of some

thought or feeling I am having in the moment.

I can STOP, become still and breathe slowly

and deeply until I feel calm again.

If my feelings are overwhelming,

I reach out and ask for help until I receive it.

There is no reason to suffer in silence.

There is nothing weak about seeking help.

I never give up on myself for any reason.

I am learning to work with my thoughts and feelings.

POWER THOUGHTS #273

I do not have to be perfect, only willing.

I am more than willing to let Spirit guide and correct me

today as I walk in peace, joy and love.

I expect things to go well today and

I align myself with a day of Grace and ease.

My inner peace is unmoved by circumstances today.

I am centered in Truth and peace as

I open to receive the gifts the Universe has for me.

Wonderful things lie ahead of me today.

POWER THOUGHT #274

I say wonderful things TO myself ABOUT myself.

There is nothing stuck-up or conceited about loving myself.

I am not comparing myself with anyone else.

I am not better or worse. I am just wonderful me.

I will be with myself forever so I am going to get along with

me and be a very good friend to myself no matter what.

I encourage myself and soothe myself every day.

I am not insecure in myself.

I know that I am a Divine Creation of Source Energy.

I do not play small or hide my light from the world.

I don't make fun of myself or of others.

I don't belittle myself to amuse others.

I am an uplifter and I love to inspire myself and others.

I believe in myself more every day and I keep encouraging

myself to be myself so that others can be themselves.

We are all freaking wonderful.

POWER THOUGHT #275

I can let go of a story that does not serve me.

I don't seek out information that will upset me.

I am not interested in gossip about others or myself.

I've decided to be a positive person.

I've decided to seek out information that uplifts me.

I can choose the stories to tell about my life

and I choose to tell the ones that feel GOOD

when I tell them, instead of focusing on unhappy facts.

I choose to focus on the positive aspects of my life and

to amplify them in order to feel good.

It is good to feel good.

I am choosing to feel good today.

POWER THOUGHTS #276

I am no longer curious about things that will upset me.

I do not need to investigate and computer search

disturbing facts and news just because they happened.

Since God is my Source, there is

no need to terrify myself with what others are doing.

I do not need to know the latest family or work gossip.

I do not need to find more reasons to be upset.

Instead, I am investigating and very curious about

what is uplifting, life-affirming, creative and positive.

I am very curious to see how many miracles

I can experience this day, this week, this month, this year.

POWER THOUGHT # 277

My life is not a popularity contest.

There are people who like me and those who don't.

That is none of my business.

I know that it is impossible to earn love or approval.

People love who they love – approve of who they choose.

It is my business to love and approve of myself.

I do my best and then let it go.

What others think of me is none of my business.

I know that I am a Child of God and

I am here for a happy Divine Purpose.

I am not here to please others.

I am here to please myself by

being Who and What God created me to be.

What others think or say about me is none of my business.

POWER THOUGHT #278

I am very slow to take offense and
very quick to forgive and let go.
I am not overly sensitive to what others say or do
because I am becoming more merciful and patient
with others and with myself.
Instead of wishing others would not push my buttons,
I am uninstalling those buttons more every day.
I am learning to let go of being offended and
I am dissolving my old defensiveness as
I choose to focus on mercy and forgiveness instead.
I am a work-in-progress, but
I am steadily moving forward as
I let Spirit heal my mind of taking offense.
I am in the process of becoming more
merciful and quick to forgive.

POWER THOUGHT #279

I forgive everyone and everyone forgives me.

I forgive myself and release myself from shame and guilt.

I always learn from my mistakes and make whatever

corrections or amends I can to anyone I may have hurt.

I forgive myself for judging and attacking myself at times.

I am now learning to be kinder and more supportive to me.

As I love and support myself, I love and support others.

What I give to myself it is easier to give to others.

I forgive and I am forgiven.

It is a new day and another opportunity to

practice the things I have learned.

I am not guilty. I am not ashamed of who I am.

I am an imperfect human, just like everyone else,

and that is a really wonderful thing to be.

I am not guilty. I am not ashamed of who I am.

I forgive and I am forgiven.

<u>POWER THOUGHT #280</u>

People are happy to see me today.

I am a beacon of joy and Light today wherever I go,

even if I don't leave my home.

I am happy to see others today and

I recognize what is good about them as

we do the dance of Life together.

People are happy to see me today

and I am happy to see them.

POWER THOUGHT #281

I am seeing what I choose to see each day.

I see people doing a good job.

I see myself thriving and improving.

I see myself growing in wisdom and patience.

I see others doing the best they can.

I see beauty in nature.

I see order in the Universe.

I see opportunities expanding.

I see things improving in so many ways.

I see miracles and amazing transformations.

I see the good in the world.

I see good in others.

I see good in myself.

I am seeing what I choose to see today.

POWER THOUGHT #282

I am releasing the illusion of control.

I cannot control the world outside of me

or what others are doing or saying.

I can only guide my own emotions and perceptions.

I choose today to give up control so

that I can *positively influence* instead of manipulating.

I let go of resisting what is happening outside of me

so that I can be at peace and respond with wisdom.

I am relaxing into the flow of Life today

as I give up the struggle of trying to control the world.

POWER THOUGHT #283

I am forever connected to an Infinite Source

Which loves, guards and guides me every hour

of the day and night, every moment of my life.

With God, all things are possible for me

as I relax and let Spirit take the lead.

I align myself with the perfect joyous

Divine Will today, so that I may rest in God.

I am forever connected to my Divine Source.

POWER THOUGHT #284

I am not here to audition for love or approval.

I am learning to love and approve of myself so that I can feel

the joyous freedom of living the life I choose.

I am grateful for being exactly who and what I am.

I appreciate myself in all my facets.

I speak only words of love and encouragement to myself.

I give myself credit for my accomplishments.

I do not hide my light under a bushel or

downplay the good that I do and have done.

I do not think I am better than anyone else, but I am equal

to anyone living on the planet today because I am a

wonderful unique expression of the Divine Source.

If people like me, cool.

If they don't, that's cool too.

I like me just fine.

<u>POWER THOUGHT #285</u>

The joy & peace within me can never be lost or taken away.

They were placed there by my Creator as eternal gifts.

This world didn't give them to me and so

the world can't take them away.

It is only possible for me to become distracted from them

if I tell myself terrifying or stressful stories,

but the joy and peace remain there waiting to be invoked.

I am invoking my eternal gifts of peace and joy today,

knowing that since the world didn't give them to me

the world can't take them away.

<u>POWER THOUGHT #286</u>

My goal is progress, not perfection.

Instead of looking at how far I have yet to go,

I focus on how far I have already come.

I may have backslid and fallen down a thousand times,

but I am only focusing on how many times I rise again.

I am continuing to go forward at my own pace

knowing there is no race, no competition, no prize to win.

I am making wonderful steady progress in

living in love, peace, joy and abundance.

POWER THOUGHT #287

I know that "lots can happen today" when

I let go of trying to manipulate how my good will come.

This is an Intelligent Universe of limitless possibilities

and I do not have to design the formula for my success.

I trust that the Universe knows just how to

line me up with the answer to every challenge

and the open door to my greater good.

Instead of focusing on obstacles,

I focus on remembering that in this limitless Universe

of miraculous possibilities, lots can happen today,

this week, this month, this year!

<u>P O W E R   T H O U G H T   # 288</u>

I am attractive and have a magnetic personality.

It may not be obvious to the world, but there is something

special and wonderful about me that others can feel

if they are the right ones for me.

I don't need a huge quantity of people because I am

focused on the quality of the people in my life.

I draw to myself the most wonderful amazing people and

our relationships are joyous and mutually beneficial.

Something in me brings out the best in other people and so

I find that I enjoy people more all the time,

even if we don't have much in common.

I live and let live because I am able to attract to me those

people who are the Divine Selection in all areas of my life.

I am attractive and have a magnetic personality.

POWER THOUGHT #289

I am quick to praise and point out the good

that I see in others instead of pointing out their errors.

I am quick to point out the good in myself

instead of pointing out and amplifying my errors.

I know that what I notice and take action on

will only grow and expand in my experience

so I am now choosing to praise and point out the good.

The good in my life is now growing and expanding

daily as I choose to praise and take action on

blessing and amplifying the good I see.

POWER THOUGHT #290

I am a visionary and a believer.

I believe in my vision for myself and for my life and I know

that my vision is the BIG YES in my world.

I say YES to MY vision for myself and that makes it easier

for me to say NO to the things that interfere with my

being who I want to be, doing what I want to do,

and having what I want to have.

I can say no to people trying to change me or to get me to

go against my own values and beliefs.

I can say no to hurting or diminishing myself.

I can say no to playing small and hiding.

I can say no to changing myself to please others.

I can say no to all of this because my vision for my life is the

BIG YES that I am moving toward more every day.

I am saying YES to my vision for my life because I believe in

my vision, I believe in my dreams, I believe in myself.

POWER THOUGHT #291

I courageously go after what I want in life.

I do not expect others to make me happy

or to read my mind about what I want.

Instead, I take responsibility for communicating what is

most important to me – what I love, what I like, what works

for me and what I want to accomplish.

I also listen to what others love, want and choose.

We can all help one another without taking responsibility

for each other's happiness or success in life.

I do not talk myself out of pursuing my dreams and goals.

I encourage myself and know that anything is possible if

I will just keep walking in the direction of my goals.

I courageously go after what I want in life, one step at a

time with determination and patience.

There is no telling how far I can go until I try.

POWER THOUGHT #292

Love is the most important thing in my life.

Every day I give and receive love in ways that matter to me.

Expressing love feels good to me.

I know that not everyone expresses love in the same way

I do and so I pay attention to learn how others

want to be loved by me.

I respect their boundaries and preferences and I let others

know what my boundaries and preferences are.

Some people are not comfortable with hugs, or touch,

or loving words, so I respect that and find out

what they DO prefer.

Each of us has our own love "language" and I am learning

how to speak the many languages of love because love is so

important for me to give and receive.

Just because someone cannot say, "I love you" does not

mean they are not feeling deep, deep love.

I let go of insisting that others act the same way I do.

I release others people from feeling as I do.

I begin by loving myself, no matter what.

Who and how others love, is their business.

POWER THOUGHT #293

I am always healing in perfect timing and ways.

The Divine Intelligence which created me

coded me as a self-healing and renewing Being.

This Intelligence radiates through every cell

of my body as Divine Wisdom and harmony.

Therefore, I am always healing and restoring

without effort or struggle.

The more I relax and get out of the way,

the more efficiently and quickly I heal and renew.

I now relax and let my Inner Wisdom take over

as I remember that I am a self-healing Being.

When I see any healing or medical professional,

I know that they are using their skills to

compliment and assist my own self-healing.

Every hand that touches me is a healing hand.

I am always healing in perfect timing and ways.

POWER THOUGHT #294

I will not torture or torment myself today.

I will not criticize or judge myself in any way.

I am giving myself a break today so that

I can experience inner peace and happiness.

I will do my best today, and that is good enough.

I let go of perfectionism.

I let go of competition.

I let go of criticism and condemnation.

I am in my own corner today, cheering myself on and

giving myself a break from the myth of perfection.

Who I am is enough.

<u>POWER THOUGHT #295</u>

I am always at the right place at the right time.

Whenever I am ready to meet someone, there they are.

Whenever anyone is ready to meet me, there I am.

I trust my Source to work out all the details so

that I can relax and let the opportunity come

when it is ripe and ready for juicy picking.

My life runs in perfect timing and order.

When I am ready, the opportunity appears.

<u>POWER THOUGHT #296</u>

I am a creative person with good ideas.

I have a wonderful mind,

whether it fits the mold of society or not.

I do not need to fit in the boxes the world has made.

I know there IS NO box – it's just an illusion made up by

people who think they know what is best for everyone.

All progress in history has been made by people who did

not fit into the mold that was set for them by others.

Some of my ideas work, and some do not.

It's okay. I'm learning to take risks and to pursue the things

that interest me even if no one else I know sees their value.

I am a creative person with interesting ideas

and ways of seeing things.

I trust myself and my process of learning and growing.

POWER THOUGHT #297

I am not a victim of my past or present.

I am not a survivor of trauma.

My body may have been victimized or traumatized but my

spirit cannot be touched or hurt in any way.

I have a body but I am not a body.

I am perfect eternal spirit.

I am a Child of the Infinite Living God of LIFE!

As such, I am a thriver and a miracle worker.

I release my past, present and future into

the Hands of God where all is blessed and healed.

Whatever horrors may have happened to me

are now being washed away by the Living Waters

of Divine Love and restoration.

I am now experiencing the healing of my mind,

and my Divine restoration to joy, sanity and inner peace.

I relax now and let this happen in perfect timing and ways.

I am thankful to God for this miracle.

I release it now for God to work out all the details

in wonderful ways for the highest good of all concerned.

And so it is. And so I let it be. Amen.

POWER THOUGHT #298

I am happy to be me today.

There is no one else I would rather be in this life.

I see my own magnificence today.

It doesn't matter whether others see it or not.

Popularity and "likes" on social media are meaningless.

Hitler was very popular in his day and

Jesus was very unpopular in his times.

What the world thinks about me is totally meaningless.

What matters is what I think about myself.

It doesn't matter what others say about me.

It matters what I say about myself, to myself.

What matters is how I treat myself and others.

Today I treat myself with enthusiastic love and joy.

Today I treat others with kindness and respect.

Today is already a great day.

POWER THOUGHT #299

There are so many wonderful amazing things

going on all over the world every single day.

The news only reports the bad and messed up things going

on across the planet, but there is much more happening

every day that is loving, generous, kind and beautiful.

I am part of that beauty today because I am choosing to

spread kindness and joy today in my own small way.

I know I will be given an opportunity to extend some love

and kindness today if I pay attention.

And I know that whatever I put out into the Universe

will come back to me in surprising and wonderful

ways if I relax and keep my heart open.

It will probably not even come from anyone I have helped

but from some unexpected person or situation.

I am a part of the wonderful things happening on the planet

today and I am making it a better place to live.

POWER THOUGHT #300

I am a prosperous person.

My parents and family are not the source

of my money or abundance – they are just one avenue

through which it comes into my world.

The Universe is the Source of all my good and there is no

lack or limitation to what I can create and receive.

I am learning to understand money and prosperity as just

one form of energy in this world.

Money is not good or bad and having or not having it

doesn't mean anything about a person.

I do not judge other people or myself based on money

or possessions or the lack of them.

I am learning about money and I know that I can trust

myself to always have enough for whatever I need.

It is only one of the ways the Universe provides for my

good, and there are many honest fun loving wonderful

ways for it to find its way into my life.

POWER THOUGHT #301

I have never been rejected. I have only been spared.

When it seems I've been rejected it is only

because somehow it was not an energy match

with the person, place or situation.

We were being spared the pain of something

that was not right at the time for our greater good.

I don't have to know or understand why it was not a good

match or did not work out the way I wanted.

I trust that my heart will heal and that there are many more

opportunities for good ahead of me – limitless good.

I release the past and know that

I have never been rejected, only spared.

POWER THOUGHT #302

I am a dreamer and a doer.

I fill my vision board with my dreams and goals,

knowing that all things are possible when I believe.

And as I continue to believe and let my vision for myself

grow and expand, I take inspired action.

I go inside myself every day to meditate on

listening to the Divine Source within me.

I may ask Source, "Is there anything I need to know?"

as I then quiet myself and tune into my intuition.

My guidance is always loving, never harmful.

My good is my own and does not take from another.

My good does not interfere with

the free will of any other person.

There is more than enough for everyone.

I believe in my dreams because I believe in myself.

POWER THOUGHT #303

My best years are still ahead of me.

I do not waste time ruminating on the past,

or worrying about the future.

I know that as I focus on the joy of this day,

my future is taking care of itself because

I am aligned with the Source of all Good.

Ahead of me is still great creativity, love, joy,

prosperity, interesting and loving relationships

with wonderful people, positive contributions

to the world and people around me and

wonderful new things to learn and master.

My best years are still ahead of me.

<u>POWER THOUGHT #304</u>

I am a very good catch.

I do not have to do anything to make someone love me.

I am not desperate and I never change my standards in

order to get someone or to keep someone in my life.

I have a lot to offer the right person and

I am not in a hurry to couple up.

It will happen in the right time in the right way.

I treat myself with love and respect and will only be with

those who also treat me with love and respect.

I take my time to think about what I want in life and then

I trust the Universe to guide and direct everything as

I remember not to rush myself or to settle for less.

I remember that I am a very good catch and there is plenty

of time for me to discover what I want in my relationships.

POWER THOUGHT #305

No one ever dies, we only change form.

No matter how many loved ones have gone on before me

we are only separate within the story of bodies.

I am forever joined with those I love as

I open my mind to make the connection.

I can feel the loving presence of those who have

made their transition to non-physical if I am

willing to not judge according to appearances.

Physical death of the body is not the end,

it is only a continuation of the spiritual journey.

I know that my journey is not over when I drop this body.

I will once again see my loved ones and we will

continue on in love together in God's perfect timing.

There is no death, only changes in form but I know that life

here in physical form is very very precious and I honor it and

intend to make the very most of my time here.

POWER THOUGHT #306

I treat others with respect and kindness because

that is how I want to be treated by others.

I do not take advantage of others, bully them,

make fun of them or gossip about them.

I do my best to focus on the good in others because it feels

better to focus on the good than the bad in life.

I focus on the positive aspects of people instead of thinking

about what may bother me about someone.

The more I focus on the good in them,

the more good they usually demonstrate with me.

But that doesn't mean I have to like everyone.

If I do not have a good vibe with someone, I can simply let

go and move on without judging or attacking them.

I can mind my own business and stay in my own mental

yard, knowing that it feels better to focus on positives.

When I judge or attack others in my mind, it makes me feel

crappy because my thoughts never leave my own mind.

Therefore, I choose to think positive, loving, respectful

thoughts of others, so that MY mind feels good.

POWER THOUGHT #307

I am learning how to express my feelings in appropriate

ways with the person it concerns directly.

It is a learning process and I know that I may make mistakes

or get embarrassed, and that is okay.

I give myself permission to be nervous while

I speak from my heart as best I can.

It's okay for me to say how I feel,

without blaming or attacking the other person.

I'm just sharing my feelings as best I can

if it is a safe space to communicate in.

I ask the person if it is okay for me to tell them how I feel.

If they are open and ready to hear it,

I center myself with my breath and share my feelings.

I know they may not respond the way I would like.

It's okay. I stay calm and centered.

I let them respond and do my best to hear with my heart.

No one is perfect at this, but I am

giving myself permission to learn as I go.

I will do the best I can as I learn to express my feelings in

appropriate ways, at appropriate times.

<u>P O W E R   T H O U G H T S   # 308</u>

I can ask for what I want in my relationships with other

people and set boundaries for what is okay and what isn't.

I am not here to meet the needs of other people.

I am here to have happy mutually beneficial friendships.

I don't allow others to take advantage of me

just to get their approval or friendship.

I respect myself, my time, my talents and my

companionship, and that means having good boundaries.

I don't need to get angry if someone is trying to manipulate

or control me, I can just let them go and walk away.

I don't manipulate others or control other people.

I respect other people and myself.

My time and friendship is worth a lot so I don't give it away

to those who will not play at the same level I do.

We all have something valuable to contribute and it is much

more fun if we are all giving of ourselves.

I choose to create healthy boundaries for myself as I learn

and grow in relationships with the world around me.

POWER THOUGHTS #309

I cannot control what other people say or think about me.

What matters is what I say and think about myself.

I am not even interested in what others say about me

because I have better things to do pursuing my interests.

Some of the most beloved successful people in the world

had difficult childhoods and were thought to be weird.

I focus my attention on what brings ME joy rather than in

trying to please the people around me.

As I learn to do the things that I enjoy, I will eventually

attract others who like me just the way I am.

What others think about me is none of my business.

Whoever others are gossiping about today will be forgotten

as soon as there is something new to judge and attack.

I have bigger dreams to pursue than trying to get the

approval of people who love to gossip.

Instead of listening to gossip, I fill my mind with positive

encouraging thoughts ABOUT MYSELF and about life.

POWER THOUGHT #310

I am not my mistakes, nor am I my past.

I am not defined by anything I do or have done.

God has defined me as a Divine Creation and

I only make mistakes when I forget that and

think of myself as a human body in a physical world.

I am a spiritual Being in a spiritual Universe.

I am remembering Who I am more every day.

The more I remember Who I am,

the more I am guided to act only from that awareness.

I am an eternal spiritual Being,

here only to joyously give and receive

the peace and blessings of God.

<u>POWER THOUGHT #311</u>

I will not stress myself out or give in to worrying.

There is a peaceful center of calmness inside me.

I will go there today whenever I need a break.

I am not here to prove myself to anyone or to meet the

expectations of anyone else.

I give myself permission to be me and to let myself grow

at my own pace and in my own way.

I let go of thinking that I know what others are thinking.

I stay in my own mental yard, thinking thoughts of self-love

and peaceful self-acceptance.

I am doing the best I can

and that is more than good enough.

I choose to think soothing thoughts about myself today.

<u>POWER THOUGHT #312</u>

I am enthusiastic about the road before me.

I have never lived this day before and

I am curious and delighted to see what

wonders Spirit has to show me.

I ask for and receive gifts from my Source today

as I open my arms wide to let in all the good!

I am a grateful gracious receiver.

POWER THOUGHT #313

I have so much to live for and so much to look forward to in this life and I have barely gotten started.

Everyone has challenges and obstacles in their lives, just as everyone has tragedy and loss along the way.

I know that there is a Spirit within me that can handle these things with help and patience and time.

I am a resilient person and there is a lot of joy and happiness ahead of me no matter what I may be going through today or even this year.

Instead of focusing on my weaknesses, I am choosing to focus on the places where I am strong and able.

Here are 3 things that I honor and appreciate about me:

_____

_____

_____

POWER THOUGHT #314

I am releasing and dissolving past hurts and limitations.

I don't have to make sense of them in order to let them go

to God to be washed away in cleansing Grace and Love.

I am letting go of the past and focusing on what there is to

appreciate about the present moments today.

I am not what happened to me in the past.

I am not my failures or mistakes and

I am not the failures or mistakes of those around me.

Right now, in this very moment, I am a Divine Child of Light.

I get to say who I am and I say I am wonderful.

I say I am powerful.

I say I am loving and kind.

I say I am an amazing work-in-progress.

I say I have many talents and gifts even if they have not yet

begun to make themselves known to me.

I am wiling to do what it takes to discover myself.

I let go of the past and look forward to what today will bring

as I focus on nurturing myself just the way I am.

POWER THOUGHT #315

All things are held perfectly in the Hands of God.

I may not like what is happening at any given moment,

but if I judge not according to appearances,

I can return to peace and sanity remembering

that right here, right now,

all things are held perfectly in the Hands of God.

I am trusting in the loving Divine Mother-Father

to lead, guide and guard me today as

I cast my cares on God-within-me.

<u>POWER THOUGHT #316</u>

I am not in competition with anyone.

I am not here to prove myself or to try to audition for love.

I am lovable because I exist, and so is everyone else.

I am worthy just as I am – there is no need to compete.

Instead, I find and discover what makes my heart sing in life
and I pursue that with a joyous passion.

I don't compare myself with what anyone else is being,
doing or having in their lives because they are not me.

I am happy for the success of others and I am happy for the
successes I am finding for myself too.

We are all in this together.

I choose to cooperate instead of competing.

POWER THOUGHT #317

Just like a car on the road going somewhere,

I can always quickly return to my highlighted route when

I have gotten off-course and lost my way.

It doesn't matter how far off-course I have gotten

or how long I have seemingly been lost,

my Divine Source has never lost contact with me.

I simply remember how I want to FEEL

and I program that into my mind as I let

Source guide me back onto my joyous journey.

The Universe can bring to me the ESSENCE of

whatever desire I have as long as I let go

of my attachment to the form of things.

What is manifested is not as important as

how I feel at any given moment and

I am choosing how I want to feel today

as I open to receive the ESSENCE of my desire.

POWER THOUGHT #318

I would rather be happy than win a debate.

I would rather be peaceful than argue for my limitations.

I would rather feel love than hold onto being right.

I would rather prove God than prove my point.

I would rather sleep well than have the last word.

I am letting go of separation and attack thoughts.

I am letting go of guilt, shame and blame as

they are gently replaced by the peace and blessings of God.

Above all else, I want the peace and joy of God today.

I release all defensiveness as I relax into the

arms of the Divine Mother where I am

bathed in the healing waters of joy, love and peace.

I am choosing and accepting the peace of God today.

POWER THOUGHT #319

I am *letting* my dreams come true instead of
trying to force or manipulate them into being.
I know that I am not dealing with a resistant Universe
which I need to convince or petition for my good.
My Source has already given EVERYTHING to me
and my job is simply to align with it and let it in.
Each day I am opening more to let my dreams come true
in their *essence*, instead of being fixated on the forms.
As I relax and trust my Source, my good is often
very different than I pictured it, but *feels* even better.
I trust my Source as I am letting
my happy dreams come true.
Whatever actions I take are inspired
by my connection to my Divine Source.
I am not struggling or manipulating –
I am showing up, prepared, on time, doing what
I said I would do, with a great attitude.
I then step back and let the Universe take over
and I happily watch the miracles happen.

POWER THOUGHT #320

I release my loved ones into Divine Care today.

I know that God's ministering Angels are tending to them.

I see them bathed in White Light and surrounded by Grace

knowing that they are held perfectly in the Hands of God.

I send them my unconditional love and acceptance

knowing that God is the Source of their good and

I am simply a vessel through which

that good sometimes flows.

I release my community, my country, and this planet

into Divine Care today knowing that God's ministering

Angels are tending to us all.

POWER THOUGHT #321

There is a champion living in my mind.

I have decided to feed the champion every day now.

I feed my mental champion by thinking encouraging loving

thoughts about myself as often as possible.

This is not about being an athlete or competitor.

There are champions in wheel chairs.

There are champions who write poetry or

love songs or computer programs.

I now awaken the champion in my mind.

It doesn't matter what anyone else on earth says about me

or to me, what matters is what I say to myself and I have

decided to say only encouraging empowering things now.

The champion in me was created by Source and there is a

champion in every person living on the planet today.

Even if I fail a hundred thousand times, my champion is still

within me urging me on to go for it again when I am ready.

This champion is not competing with anyone – it is not a

contest and there is no one to race against.

The champion in me recognizes the champion in others and

we uplift and inspire each other to be who we really are.

I am a champion, living in a world of champions.

POWER THOUGHT #322

I know that growth and change can be messy,

uncomfortable and even overwhelming at times.

It's okay. I am safe. It's only change.

No one whips through puberty in 15 minutes

or has it all together all the time.

It is ridiculous to compare my insides to someone else's

outside because I have no idea of what anyone is really

going through or what they are dealing with.

My growth process is my own and I am learning to be

patient and gentle with myself as it unfolds.

We all have daily challenges and lessons to learn.

I let go of perfectionistic thinking

and impatience with myself and my life.

Whatever I'm going through is okay.

I will ask for help when I need help.

I have compassion for myself and others.

We are all doing the best we can and

there is no rush about any of this.

I am safe. It's only change.

POWER THOUGHT #323

Sometimes I am afraid, and that is okay.

No one on earth is without fear at times.

Now when I feel fear, instead of resisting it,

I ask the fear what it is trying to tell me.

I talk to it soothingly like I would a little kid.

I am learning to understand myself and that

some fears are rational because they come

from my inner wisdom and intuition.

Many other fears are not rational and need me

to gently soothe them into subsiding.

Fear of playing on the freeway is rational.

Fear of speaking in public is not rational and can be

gradually, gently soothed, dissolved and released.

We all have fear. It's okay.

I am learning to talk to my fears and find out what they are

trying to tell me so that I can live with more joy.

I can share my fears with my mentors, leaders or other

people who are trustworthy and have more wisdom and life

experience and let them help me to find my own answers.

There is NO SHAME in being afraid.

I can ask for and receive help when I am afraid.

<u>POWER THOUGHT #324</u>

I am learning how to express my feelings appropriately.

Sometimes I say things that hurt other people

or that hurt me in some way. This is not what I want.

No one communicates perfectly all the time, but I am

learning how to communicate my feelings by thinking about

how what I say may make the other person feel.

I am learning how to express my feelings without attacking

or being defensive, but it is a process and I am willing to be

patient with myself and the people around me as we learn.

I am letting go of guilt, blame and shame to see the real

feeling that is underneath them.

I know I have a good heart and I want to share this heart

with others who will honor it and who are trustworthy.

Therefore, I am in the process of learning how to

communicate in ways that allow me to say what is true for

me, while LISTENING to what others are trying to tell me.

I seek not only to be understood by others,

but to understand those around me as well.

It is a two-way street.

I am learning how to express my feelings appropriately.

POWER THOUGHT #325

I've decided not to judge myself today.

I've decided not to judge anyone else today.

Instead, I am giving us all a freaking break!

I will dissolve all attack and judging thoughts by

remembering that everyone gets a break today.

I am giving us all the benefit of the doubt and assuming that

anyone who is acting awful is probably doing so because of

some personal problem of which I am not aware.

It doesn't excuse bad behavior, but I am not going to make

myself feel awful by judging and attacking them.

For my own peace of mind, I am giving us all a break today.

<u>POWER THOUGHT #326</u>

I love and bless my body exactly as it is right now.
I release and dissolve any resistance or judgments
I may have about this wonderful body since
I know that it is a Divine Creation of the One Source.
It is the perfect size and shape for me today.
If there is any pain or discomfort in it,
I breathe in God's merciful kindness to that
part of it and I relax knowing that there is
nothing to get rid of, nothing to battle or fight.
My body is a precious gift and
I now choose to love and bless it just as it is.
I forgive myself if I have ever mistreated or abused it.
I forgive it for any judgments I have had against it.
I am now blessing my body and giving it to God
to joyfully manage and use for miracles.
I love and appreciate my beautiful body.

POWER THOUGHT #327

There is nothing to fear.

I have a Spiritual Guide/Angel to always help me.

I know that my Guide walks with me and directs me today

to the extent that I turn within and seek help.

Whatever happens, I am not alone and I have all the

Help I need to move through conditions in clarity and peace.

If I am afraid, it is only because I have forgotten my Guide

and am trusting in my own human strength instead of

leaning on the everlasting arms of my Divine Companion.

I let go of judging according to appearances as

I am now trusting in my Companion to walk me

through everything that comes my way today.

<u>POWER THOUGHT #328</u>

I am counting my blessings instead of counting my worries.

The vision of one world costs me the vision of the other.

Therefore, I am choosing to focus on the world of blessings.

It is up to me which direction I will look in –

the one of pain and sorrow, or the one of

miracles, love and limitless Light.

There is plenty of evidence for both worlds

but I cannot see both at the same time.

I am focusing on just how good I have it today.

I am focusing on how much more good is ahead.

I am counting my blessings today.

POWER THOUGHT #329

There is no rush in my growth and learning process.

There are some people who are still learning

and growing at 97 years of age.

I am taking the pressure off myself.

I am seeing life as a grand adventure of lifelong discovery.

Each of us has our own unique path and unfolding.

It is full of mistakes and victories.

I am not defined by any one mistake or any one victory.

The most successful people have often

had the most failures as well.

The point is to learn from them all and to keep exploring.

I am a lifelong explorer and my journey has barely begun.

This is another great day to learn and grow.

I look forward to seeing what unfolds today.

POWER THOUGHT #330

I have limitless resources at my disposal because I am
connected to a limitless Divine Source.

If I can imagine it, the Universe can deliver it.

I am not dependent on my family or on any humans to
receive the bounty of the Universe.

The Source of my good is within me and in my own
Consciousness and alignment with the limitless.

There is no shortage of money or time.

The Universe is always creating more and more.

I am part of the Universe and am therefore part of the
limitless creation of more and more.

My part is to BELIEVE in myself and my dreams even when
I have no idea HOW they will come to pass.

I listen to my own inner Guidance and let it line me up with
the right people, places, things and right actions.

I have limitless resources at my disposal.

<u>POWER THOUGHT #331</u>

Wonderful synchronicity is happening more

frequently in my life all the time.

I seem to show up just when the good things

are starting and the right doors are opening for me.

The more I relax and enjoy my life,

the more these wonderful things happen.

I can do what needs to be done today without being

stressed out and hard on myself or others.

I can calmly get in the flow of things moving forward while

I do what needs to get done.

As I do this, I align with the Universal Source which makes

the flowers grow and the earth keep spinning.

I am not missing out on anything because where

I am is always the right place at the right time.

It's wonderful to watch how my life is choreographed

to meet up with so many wonderful experiences

and people as I simply tune into my own Guidance.

<u>POWER THOUGHT #332</u>

Each day I am relaxing more into the receptive mode.

At this moment, there is nothing to get, or fix or change.

Instead, I am opening to receive the gifts being given.

My heart and mind are receptive to the Divine Presence

and I am being healed, soothed and uplifted as

I align myself with the love, peace and joy of God

that is so freely and abundantly given me.

I am relaxing into the receptive mode today.

POWER THOUGHT #333

I expect to have a wonderful day today.

I expect miracles to light my way.

I expect to be guided and led by Spirit.

I expect things to go well for me.

I expect love to flow to me and through me.

I expect to feel good in my body.

I expect to be inspired and guided.

I expect to receive gifts from my Source.

I expect to have wonderful interactions

with people in my world today.

I expect to be joyfully used by God to help.

I expect to prosper and thrive.

I expect a Divine Answer to any problem.

I expect things to unfold wonderfully before me.

I expect laughter and fun to flow.

I expect to have a wonderful day today.

POWER THOUGHT #334

It is easier and easier for me to see the good in people.

It is easier and easier for me to see the good in myself.

It is easier and easier for me to see the good in life.

I am appreciating life more each day as

I increase my focus on gratitude and appreciation.

As I shift my focus to the good,

the good offers itself to me at every turn.

There is a Divine Something that is responding to

my thoughts, attitudes and words.

The more I focus on the good,

the more good this Divine Something shows me.

POWER THOUGHT #335

I am seeing a bright future for myself.

No matter what my past has been,

and no matter what my present is right now,

I am not limited by any of it.

I allow myself to envision a bright happy future for myself

and I know that all things are possible for me.

I may have no idea at all how all this will happen but

I continue to imagine it and believe in it.

I don't need anyone to save me or do it for me, but I know

that I will meet many angels along the way to help me.

My part is to believe in myself and my vision.

If I can SEE it in my mind, I can hold it in my hand one day.

I am seeing a bright future for myself.

<u>POWER THOUGHT #336</u>

I have all the wonderful help I need.

I do not tell a "poor me" story because I know that

my Source gives me all the help I need if I will

simply align myself with the story of "blessed me" instead.

I am not afraid to ask for help and assistance.

I realize that people love to help and that

everyone is free to say "yes" or "no" without guilt.

I release everyone to do as they choose,

knowing that Spirit is bringing me into alignment

with all the right people and resources now.

I need not worry or scheme.

I have all the wonderful help I need

as I tell the story of "blessed blessed me!"

POWER THOUGHT #337

It's totally okay to be "weird."

I don't judge myself or others by some silly standard that

the world has set for how people should or shouldn't be.

I am learning to accept myself and accept others just as we

are, even if we all have very different ways of being.

I can live and let live.

If others think I am weird, so what?

I'm having fun discovering who I am and what works for me.

The more I appreciate myself just as I am, the more

I attract others who appreciate me just as I am.

There is room for lots and lots of variety in this world.

It's okay if other people don't always "get me" or appreciate

me because I don't always get everyone else.

I can bless and appreciate others without being like them.

I am more interested in understanding myself as I discover

all the wonderful things about myself.

POWER THOUGHT #338

I am learning to be very kind to myself and

that allows me to be kinder with others.

There is no value at all in punishing or criticizing myself.

I would rather take a positive approach to growing.

I don't criticize myself when I make mistakes but instead see

it as a valuable learning process.

I am not afraid to look silly or foolish while I am learning

new things because everybody has to start somewhere.

No one is good at everything and if

I am not good at something and don't enjoy it,

I do not attack or criticize myself.

I do my best and let it go.

I have given up all self-criticism and am learning to treat

myself with love and kindness no matter what.

POWER THOUGHT #339

If there is no one in my world right now who I relate to,

it just means that I haven't yet met people of my tribe.

We will meet eventually, but in the meantime I can learn to

appreciate people of other tribes and different ways of

being than the ways I prefer.

I am not wrong and they are not wrong.

Different does not mean wrong or bad – it's just different.

I may not even seem like anyone in my own family,

but we can still love and enjoy each other a lot.

There are so many different ways of seeing and being.

I can totally appreciate the way I am while still appreciating

those who seem extremely different than me.

We're all just visiting this planet anyhow so why not

enjoy the variety and many different ways

of being while we're here?

I am learning to consider and appreciate lots of different

ways of being in the world as I love and appreciate myself.

I can have friends who are extremely different than I am

without changing myself or my own values and tastes.

POWER THOUGHT #340

My body knows exactly what to do to bring itself

into alignment and balance no matter what the issue.

There is no such thing as impossible or incurable

for my Infinite Divine Source.

I am living in wonderful times because there are many

different ways of healing and helping the body with more

being revealed all the time.

There is no such thing as a "right" or "normal" body.

That is just a silly myth.

My body does not have to look like anyone else's.

It does not have to act or respond like anyone else's.

I am learning to trust the wisdom of my own body as

I listen to it instead of criticizing or attacking it.

I treat it with love and kindness so that it can find

its own balance and alignment.

My body is an amazing gift from the Source and I will not be

ungrateful by attacking or criticizing such a gift.

I trust the wisdom of my wonderful body.

POWER THOUGHT #341

I don't play "poor me" – instead
I play "<u>that's for me</u>!"
When I see someone in my life or in the world being, doing
or having something I would like to experience or have,
I don't get jealous or resentful or feel sorry for myself.
I remember that I live in a limitless Universe and that
I am connected to an Infinite Source.
I am not trying to steal someone else's good and my good
does not diminish the resources of anyone else.
Therefore, I align myself with this Limitless Source and say,
"<u>That's for me too</u>!" I too can thrive in love, joy, health,
prosperity, success, and all the good I see in the world.
I lift my vibration by aligning myself with the life I want
because anytime I see what I would like to experience I say,
THAT'S FOR ME TOO!
I can be who I want to be.
I can do what I want to do.
I can have what I want to have.
All things are possible when I believe.

POWER THOUGHT #342

I am able to speak my truth with ease.

I am not here to please others or to

bow to the pressure of the expectations of anyone

or anything outside of me.

My truth is *my* truth.

There is no value in me being phony or

in swallowing my true thoughts and feelings.

It is of no benefit to anyone for me to

hold myself down or to squelch who I am.

I am able to lovingly speak my truth with ease.

POWER THOUGHT #343

Loving myself allows me to prosper and grow.

As I give myself permission to love myself,

it inspires others to love and accept themselves.

I know that the way I treat myself is then

reflected back to me through others.

Other people will treat me the way I treat myself.

I am loving and respecting myself more than ever

and I see it reflected back to me as others do the same.

<u>POWER THOUGHT #344</u>

I never feel sorry for myself because I know that eventually

I will come out on the other side if I keep on going forward.

No one has a perfect life or perfect circumstances.

Everyone has challenges, failures and losses.

I don't pity myself, but I can take time to grieve and be

gentle with myself when I experience a loss or when

something I wanted does not go the way I wanted it to.

But I do not dwell in it for long or give up on myself.

I don't give up on my dreams.

Even if someone I love has died, I know that they would not

want me to give up on myself and my dreams.

When I experience loss or failure or disappointment,

I give myself time to heal but I still love and encourage

myself all through the process.

I don't need life to be perfect or to always get what

I want in order to be happy and peaceful.

I am growing stronger all the time as I remember that

I have a Divine Source within me that is

closer than breathing, nearer than hands and feet.

I am never alone. I will always rise up again.

<u>POWER THOUGHT #345</u>

I treat myself as a valuable precious treasure.

I am as God created me and I am exactly

what I was meant to be.

There is a beautiful Light within me that holds and

protects me all through the day and night.

Nothing and no one can diminish this

perfect spirit that I am.

There are no words or actions from outside of me

that can change this beautiful beam of light which I am.

From this day on I will not harm myself in any way

in thoughts, words, or actions.

I treat myself as a valuable precious treasure.

POWER THOUGHT # 346

I am surrounded by unseen angels who

love and watch over me.

They guide me to where I can do the most good

and where I can receive the most blessings.

I am a unique person in the Universe and no one

can take my place or fill the role I came to play.

I came to give and receive the peace & blessings of God.

I am lifted above the petty squabbles of the world as

Grace guides me in fulfilling my role of living from

my Center of Truth, love, kindness and mercy.

I am giving and receiving the blessings of God.

POWER THOUGHT #347

I release my family and loved ones into Divine Care.

IN THE THEATER OF MY MIND I SEE THEM THRIVING.

I SEE THEM HAPPY, HEALTHY AND LOVED.

They are blessed and embraced by Divine Love.

All their needs are taken care of this very day.

Their bodies and health are sustained by Source.

They are filled with vital energy.

Their finances come from Divine Supply.

They tap into the limitless Universal resources for

their abundant life, prosperity and happiness.

Joy fills their hearts and their minds are clear & calm.

They are safe from harm and free from fear.

Their good cannot be denied for it comes from God.

I forgive and release us from any past hurts.

We are encircled by the light of

deep forgiveness and acceptance.

We now step into a dynamic loving present

as we see one another in the Light of God's Love.

POWER THOUGHT #348

As I go to bed at night, I let go of the day behind me.

I deeply relax and let my body draw nourishment

from the Universal Source of Life.

My sleep is restful and healing.

My body and mind relax and let go.

My dreams are peaceful and nourishing

and I am guided by Angels to the Higher Realms.

As I sleep, my family and loved ones are

all held safely in the arms of God.

I am healing and renewing every night

as I sleep and rest in God.

POWER THOUGHT #349

I am shining brightly today.

All the brightest and best within me

is brought forward this day.

The Universal Light shines brightly in me

and radiates out into all that I do or say.

My thoughts are high, my spirit soars,

and my heart is open wide.

I breathe deeply and release all tension.

Any anxiety dissolves into Divine Confidence.

I give myself to the Source of all good to be joyously used to

bring more Light, fun and joy to the world through me.

I don't decide who or when or how this happens.

I am led and guided by the Spirit within me

and it is a great adventure in sharing miracles.

I am shining brightly today.

POWER THOUGHT #350

I deserve to be fairly compensated for my work.

I show up, prepared, on time, doing what I said I would do,

with a good attitude and do an excellent job.

I give respect to those I work with and for and I have high

integrity and honesty in all that I do.

Therefore, I allow myself to earn very good money and

other good compensation for what I do.

As I get better and better at what I do, my income keeps

increasing and going higher and higher.

Playing the money game is very fun for me.

I am learning how to circulate money so that I am always

giving and receiving it with joy and ease.

There is nothing wrong or evil about money

and it is not hard to get or have.

I spend some, save some, give some.

Money comes to me frequently in expected and unexpected

ways because I have made friends with money.

POWER THOUGHT #351

I envision a world of love and harmony.

I know that all Life is cradled in God's loving arms.

Divine Love is now flowing through every country and

nation as every living being is embraced in peace.

There is no poverty, pain, sickness nor lack in God.

This is an abundant Universe and there are more

than enough resources for everyone to

have all that they need to thrive and grow.

Each person is now drawing to them all

that they need in order to be happy,

healthy, safe and loved.

Greed, addictions, anger, prejudice and sickness

all dissolve in the miracle of Divine Restoration.

The citizens and leaders of every nation are now

being awakened to the truth of our Oneness.

All beings everywhere are being lifted up

to their highest and best.

We recognize the sacredness of life.

We are all healed together.

We are joyfully used to shine the Light.

And so it is.

POWER THOUGHT #352

I can <u>enjoy</u> my work.

I am letting go of any belief that I must struggle and suffer

in order to thrive and do well in the world.

I know that I can have a balance of work and play.

My work can be just as satisfying and joyous as the time

I spend with my friends and loved ones.

I am a creative individual and I have a Divine Source which

draws to me all the ideal resources to help me create a life

that I enjoy and that brings me great satisfaction.

As I pursue the things in life that interest me and feed my

passion, I know that I will find my right place in the world.

I do not have to suffer and struggle in order to prove my

worth or to thrive and do well.

I can enjoy my work as much as my play and rest.

POWER THOUGHT #353

I am training myself to focus on the good in life.

I may not like everyone who comes into my life, but I can

get along with most anyone if I focus on the good in them.

There is good in even those who upset me the most.

Instead of focusing on resentments and judgments,

I do lists of positive aspects of those I have problems with.

The more I see the good in them, the more I am actually

calling it forth and making myself feel better.

The more I resist and judge them, the more they will be in

my face and the more people just like them I will see.

I want to FEEL GOOD, so I've decided to focus on the good

in all the people around me and in myself.

It doesn't mean I have to become friends with someone

I don't like, but I can feel better by releasing them from my

attack thoughts and no longer keeping track of what I do

not like about them or what they are doing.

I can live and let live.

P O W E R   T H O U G H T   # 354

I seek out good news and the things that will inspire me.

No one is responsible for cheering me up or

putting me in a good mood.

I am responsible for my own emotional journey.

No one is coming to save me or make me feel good.

That is <u>MY</u> job and I CAN do it very well.

This is wonderful news because I am the only one who

really knows what will soothe and uplift me.

I don't wait for someone else to do it for me.

And as I take responsibility for making myself feel good in

healthy and loving ways, I create a positive momentum.

As I surround myself with what inspires and uplifts me,

I find that I attract more that inspires and uplifts me.

Life is a big mirror that reflects me back to me.

When I uplift myself, others uplift me too.

When I withhold from myself, others withhold from me too.

I am learning to treat myself the way I want to be treated

instead of wishing that others would do it for me.

I do unto myself as I would have others do unto me.

It's a great system.

<u>POWER THOUGHT #355</u>

Every day I write down at least

3 things that I did well that day.

I write down 3 good things that happened that day.

I write down 3 things I appreciate about myself.

I write down 3 things I appreciate about my loved ones.

The more I appreciate, the more there is to appreciate.

The more I appreciate, the better and better I feel.

POWER THOUGHT #356

I don't wish or hope, <u>I decide</u>.

Wishing doesn't make anything so.

Deciding is what gets the energy of Life moving.

As I do my research, think things through, consider the

consequences of my decision, ask for guidance from

mentors and consult the intuition in my gut,

I am becoming better at making good decisions and

following through with them.

Making good decisions doesn't mean I know HOW it will all

happen or how I will accomplish it.

It is simply the first positive step in moving forward.

When I make a real decision, things start to happen!

Instead of wishing and hoping, I am getting more

comfortable making good decisions.

<u>POWER THOUGHT #357</u>

I like myself more all the time.

I do not have to be perfect to like myself.

My loved ones, friends and even my pets are not perfect

and yet I love them deeply and completely.

I can like and love myself just as I am and just as I am not.

The more I like myself, the more others like me.

The more I like myself, the more I like others.

If someone doesn't like me, it has no effect

on how I feel about myself.

I let it go and move on knowing we are

just not a vibrational match to be friends.

I can even make positive changes in myself and in my habits

without attacking or judging who I am.

I can do it all from love.

POWER THOUGHT #358

I clearly and calmly ask for what I want in life.

I don't hint or try to get someone to read my mind.

I courageously and clearly ask directly of the person

who is able to give it to me instead of trying to figure out

a way to do it without putting myself out there.

The more I put myself out there, the more I get what I want.

I don't even mind hearing "no" because it saves me time

and I can move on to the next person or situation.

The people who ask for the most, get the most.

I ask without whining or trying to guilt anyone into anything

because I know that I am worthy of what I want in life.

If I don't ask, I don't get. And because I want to create a

wonderful life for myself, I ask directly for what I want.

If other people do not like that, that's okay.

I'm not being pushy – I'm being clear and direct.

It makes life a LOT easier in the long run to

ask for what I want clearly and directly.

If they say no, at least I know and we've saved time.

I give myself permission to ask for what I want in life.

POWER THOUGHT #359

It brings me great joy to help others and to make a positive

difference in their lives and in the world.

However, I do not have to do it for them or take

responsibility for their happiness.

I give and help because it feels good!

I don't allow anyone to "guilt me" into helping them.

I do it freely because I WANT to, or I don't do it.

We all need help in this life and always will.

That does not make any of us weak or

less than anyone else in the world.

We are not dependent or independent.

We are inter-dependent.

We all need each other in order to live and thrive.

When I help others, I am helping myself too.

I help where I want to when I want to,

because it feels good and feeds my soul.

Every word of encouragement I give to another,

encourages me and uplifts me.

Everything I give comes back to me multiplied.

As I give and help, I receive.

<u>P O W E R   T H O U G H T   # 360</u>

I am telling my truth with love and clarity.

I do not have to argue or debate anyone.

I stand lovingly in my own truth and

do not need to defend or explain it

to those who would not understand.

I release others to stand in their truth

even when it does not align with my own.

We are all free to think and believe as we choose.

I do not need others to agree or approve

of how I choose to express or live my life.

I am telling my truth with love and clarity.

POWER THOUGHT #361

I am taking better care of myself all the time.

I know that there is no one coming to save me -

no one who has been put in charge of my good.

I'm the one. I must save myself, and <u>I can with help</u>.

Others can help me help myself,

but ultimately it is my job.

I am saved from anxiety, stress and misery

by aligning myself with the Divine Source

and then taking action to treat myself

with loving-kindness and support.

I am responsible for me.

I am responsible for my happiness.

I am responsible for my thoughts.

I am choosing to put myself at the top of my list

for if I do not take care of myself,

I will not be of any use to anyone else.

There is nothing holy about depleting myself

or living like a beggar at the gate.

I am a Child of God and worthy of care.

I am taking better care of myself all the time.

<u>POWER THOUGHT #362</u>

I am authentically myself.

There is no one just like me.

I was created by Source as a unique individual.

I am a beautiful person, inside and out.

I am an instrument of Divine Love, healing & creativity.

I do not compare myself with anyone else.

I am not trying to fit in anywhere.

I draw to me those who appreciate me as I am.

I belong wherever I stand.

I have a right to exist.

I am authentically myself.

POWER THOUGHT #363

Age is nothing but a number.

Young and old are just concepts.

I will never stop learning and growing.

The end of one phase is the beginning of another one.

I can start fresh even at 90 or 100 years young if I choose.

All things are possible in God and I live in God.

I can begin with tiny "penguin steps" to go

in the direction of any dream or goal I have.

Nothing is stopping me but a story in my head.

I am now telling a story of possibilities

and wonderful new doors opening for me.

I am an ageless spirit in a world

of limitless possibilities and miracles.

POWER THOUGHT #364

I open myself to this wonderful new day.

I do not know what is going to happen and so

I allow Divine Spirit to guide me and

to unfold all things in perfect order and timing.

Today I remember to praise and acknowledge

the people in my life with words & actions.

I am a grateful Child of God today.

Divine activity fills my day and runs my life.

I open my heart to give and receive love.

I open myself to this wonderful new day.

POWER THOUGHT #365

I am enough, just as I am.

I am not too much, nor to little.

I am wonderful, wonderful me!

I am focusing on what is really important today.

There is no need to strive for the myth of perfection.

It is okay if not everything gets done today.

The real perfection is not in outer accomplishments

or getting everything checked off a list.

Perfection is the eternal Light within us all.

I show up, prepared, on time, doing what I said

I would do, with a good attitude –

the rest is out of my control.

There is nothing I need do to deserve my good.

My worth is established by God, not by deeds.

I do my best, and forget the rest.

I am enough, just as I am.

NOTES

Jacob Glass is an author, spiritual teacher, mentor
and mad mystic. To order his other books,
see his live class schedule, watch online videos or receive his
weekly class recordings, see his website: jacobglass.com

Made in the USA
Middletown, DE
13 December 2019